ALSO BY JOHN H. RICHARDSON

My Father the Spy: An Investigative Memoir

*In the Little World: A True Story
of Dwarfs, Love, and Trouble*

The Vipers' Club

LUIGI

The **MAKING** and the **MEANING**

JOHN H. RICHARDSON

SIMON & SCHUSTER

New York   Amsterdam/Antwerp   London   Toronto
Sydney/Melbourne   New Delhi

Simon & Schuster
1230 Avenue of the Americas
New York, NY 10020

First Simon & Schuster hardcover edition November 2025

SIMON & SCHUSTER and colophon are registered trademarks of Simon & Schuster, LLC

Simon & Schuster strongly believes in freedom of expression and stands against censorship in all its forms. For more information, visit BooksBelong.com.

For information about special discounts for bulk purchases, please contact Simon & Schuster Special Sales at 1-866-506-1949 or business@simonandschuster.com.

The Simon & Schuster Speakers Bureau can bring authors to your live event. For more information or to book an event, contact the Simon & Schuster Speakers Bureau at 1-866-248-3049 or visit our website at www.simonspeakers.com.

Interior design by Carly Loman

Manufactured in the United States of America

1 3 5 7 9 10 8 6 4 2

ISBN 978-1-6682-0934-9
ISBN 978-1-6682-0936-3 (ebook)

LUIGI

AUTHOR'S NOTE

I very much believe that Luigi is innocent until proven guilty, and I condition any speculation in the following pages on that righteous legal scruple.

CONTENTS

MAGIC ISLAND

Let's start with Luigi Mangione on that beach near Waikiki in the fall of 2022. Staring at the waves he couldn't surf, back in pain, big hungry brain swimming with ideas. He posted one online and pinned it to the top of his feed:

> 7 years ago, I gave my hs senior speech on this topic: "Today, I will be talking to you about the future, about topics ranging from conscious artificial intelligence to human immortality . . ."

This was the speech he gave as his class's valedictorian, literally speaking for his generation. Changes were coming like nothing the world had ever seen, he promised. "When we understand just how fast the rate of human progress is increasing, a revolutionary near future isn't unbelievable, it's actually the only logical conclusion."

His advice: "Be excited for what the future holds for us."

Seen from two and a half years later, this was a moment of touching optimism. He still believed in the power of knowledge to change things, still had a sense that history was moving forward in positive ways. He had a six-figure job too, working as a data engineer at an online car dealer called TrueCar.com. There, according to his LinkedIn page, he "spearheaded the transition and integration of lease/loan payments to a new API [a software interface], expanded pricing data sources, and improved call frequency and conditions, resulting in a 34% increase in new vehicle payments populated and more up-to-date payments."

He spent his first six months in Hawaii in a shared living space called Surfbreak, a high-rise right by the water, with surfboards on a rack and communal spaces filled with attractive young people, then rented an apartment in another high-rise along with an office nearby. He spent his spare time hiking, rock climbing, working out and doing yoga. He even started a book club with his Surfbreak friends that focused on social issues, reading books like Tim Urban's *What's Our Problem? A Self-Help Book for Societies* and Steve Stewart-Williams's *The Ape That Understood the Universe: How the Mind and Culture Evolve.* They'd spend afternoons talking them through out on Magic Island, a stunning beach that takes in the curve of Waikiki Beach with its hotels and Diamond Head crowning above. Luigi was a thoughtful reader, club members said later, gifted at parsing the nuances of an argument.

Then that book club decided to read Theodore John Kaczynski's *Industrial Society and Its Future,* also known as the Unabomber Manifesto. It wasn't even Luigi's idea, and there are so many reasons that a person with his background should have hated it, from his degrees in computer science to the robot- and video game–designing clubs he started in high school and college to any higher ambitions he might ever want to pursue in the field he had studied. This is how it begins:

The industrial revolution and its consequences have been a disaster for the human race. They have greatly increased the life-expectancy of those of us who live in "advanced" countries, but they have destabilized society, have made life unfulfilling, have subjected human beings to indignities, have led to widespread psychological suffering (in the Third World to physical suffering as well) and have inflicted severe damage on the natural world.

Written in 232 numbered sections, like an instruction manual for some immense tool, the manifesto has two main themes. First, technology's dark momentum can't be stopped. With each improvement, the graceful schooner that sails our shorelines becomes the hulking mega-tanker that takes our jobs. Cars are a blast when bouncing along dirt roads at the reckless speed of twenty miles per hour, but pretty soon we're stuck in rush-hour traffic, producing our license and registration and paying down car loans. We doze off while exploring a fun new thing called social media and wake up to Big Data, fake news and Total Information Awareness. And that isn't even getting started with massive existential bureaucracies like the health care system. It's all too big, too fast, too much.

The manifesto's second theme is that we've become so dependent on technology that the real decisions about our lives are made by unseen forces like corporations and market flows that feel like conspiracies even when they're not. Our lives are modified to fit the needs of these forces and the diseases of modern life are the result: "Boredom, demoralization, low self-esteem, inferiority feelings, defeatism, depression, anxiety, guilt, frustration, hostility, spouse or child abuse, insatiable hedonism, abnormal sexual behavior, sleep disorders, eating disorders, etc."

As many have said, these ideas aren't new. They're in movies like *The Matrix*, *I Am Legend*, *Avatar*, and *Wall-E*, even *Fern-Gully: The Last Rainforest*. They're in books like *The Road* and *Parable of the Sower*. We live in a world where tech tycoons build bugout estates in New Zealand, smartphone executives refuse to let their kids use smartphones and data miners find ways to hide their own data. But Kaczynski wasn't a filmmaker or a novelist or a climate scientist with carefully expressed concerns. He was a math genius who went to Harvard at sixteen and made breakthroughs in "boundary functions," which has something to do with measuring curves in three dimensions. He joined the mathematics department at UC Berkeley when he was just twenty-five, the youngest hire in the university's ninety-nine-year history. With economic prose and a ruthlessly matter-of-fact tone, he looks at the facts and comes to the logical conclusion, which he offers with the serene detachment of HAL, the computer in *2001: A Space Odyssey*:

> The bigger the system grows the more disastrous the results of its breakdown will be, so if it is to break down it had best break down sooner rather than later. We therefore advocate a revolution against the industrial system.

He doesn't mince words on methods, either:

> Power depends ultimately on physical force. By teaching people that violence is wrong (except, of course, when the system itself uses violence via the police or the military), the system maintains its monopoly on physical force and thus keeps all power in its own hands.

This was too much for the book club. Most of the other readers hadn't wanted to read *Industrial Society and Its Future* in the first place. The club broke up.

Luigi's reaction to the manifesto didn't seem especially positive either. At least that's the take from R. J. Martin, another member of the club: "Nothing that stood out at the time. No anger. No special affinity towards it. Just, you know, thought-provoking discussion."

Kaczynski's manifesto actually has a lot in common with *What's Our Problem?* Tim Urban, also the creator of a popular blog called *Wait But Why*, opens his book on an even more alarming version of Kaczynski's premise—that technology is not just growing but growing exponentially, moving faster and faster as it gets bigger and bigger. After 240,000 years as hunter-gatherers surviving on the fruits of nature and another 12,000 years developing agriculture, he says, we spent just 250 years developing modern technology, and all of a sudden we've got the internet, cell phones and modern medicine but also the atomic bomb, bioweapons, genetic engineering and AI so powerful it could destroy the world. If we get things right, Urban says, life could be "unfathomably awesome." If not, "this might be the last page of the story."

Urban's book ends on a cheery note, trusting in the eternal power of human courage and ingenuity. Luigi gave it the ultimate rave: "I believe this book will go down in history as one of the most important philosophical texts of the early 21st century."

But he couldn't stop thinking about Kaczynski's manifesto, and changes were coming at him one after another. A surfing accident aggravated his long-standing back problems, putting him in frequent pain for over a year. He quit his job at TrueCar early in 2023, telling a friend it was mind-numbingly dull. In July, he flew to the East Coast for back surgery.

By this time, his reading list included books like *Merchants of Doubt: How a Handful of Scientists Obscured the Truth on Issues from Tobacco Smoke to Global Warming*, by Naomi Oreskes and Erik M. Conway, and Bill Gates's *How to Avoid Climate Disaster: The Solutions We Have and the Breakthroughs We Need*. One day, he reposted a photo of an old, yellowed newspaper clipping from 1912:

> The furnaces of the world are now burning about 2,000,000,000 tons of coal a year. When this is burned, uniting with oxygen, it adds about 7,000,000,000 tons of carbon dioxide to the atmosphere yearly. This tends to make the air a more effective blanket for the earth and to raise its temperature. The effect may be considerable in a few centuries.

He retweeted posts about AI, which he had studied at Penn and taught to high school students at Stanford in the summer of 2019. AI worried him, but it was amazing too. He retweeted a thread about the fall of Rome that blamed it on an "unsustainable welfare state" where people ate for free and spent all their time at the Coliseum. "Out of 365 days, more than 200 were public holidays and 93 were 'devoted to games at the public expense.'" The thread ended on a cliff-hanger: "As welfare states expand around the world today, and entertainment options get ever more immersive, we are forced to ask a question: Is this Post-Industrial Civilization Rome, Part II?"

He worried about men. His reading list included Richard V. Reeves's *Of Boys and Men: Why the Modern Male Is Struggling,*

Why It Matters, and What to Do About It. He retweeted a video from a British online influencer named Jess Gill: "It's sad that the question of 'are men important?' can't be answered with a simple 'yes.' What message does this send to young boys when society says that they're good at nothing?"

On X, he retweeted a lengthy post by a woman calling herself Daughter of Wolves:

> If you want to understand men better, just look at all the movies they've made, books they've written, and games they invent when they're young.
>
> Almost every single one is about a young man being thrust into a position or situation he doesn't know if he can overcome. Many times he actually believes he can't, so he initially refuses the challenge . . .
>
> In the end, he rises above, he wins, he conquers. He conquers first himself and then he conquers the threat.

Her conclusion: Men are made for impossible heroic feats, and women should encourage them.

On January 23, 2024, Luigi finally posted his review of the Unabomber Manifesto:

> Clearly written by a mathematics prodigy. Reads like a series of lemmas* on the question of 21st century quality of life.
>
> It's easy to quickly and thoughtless [sic] write this off as the manifesto of a lunatic, in order to avoid facing some of the

---

* *Lemma* is a math term for a kind of proposition.

uncomfortable problems it identifies. But it's simply impossible to ignore how prescient many of his predictions about modern society turned out.

He was a violent individual—rightfully imprisoned—who maimed innocent people. While these actions tend to be characterized as those of a crazy luddite, however, they are more accurately seen as those of an extreme political revolutionary.

Then he quoted an "interesting" post he had found online by a Reddit user called Bosspotatoness:

Had the balls to recognize that peaceful protest has gotten us absolutely nowhere, and at the end of the day he's probably right. Oil barons haven't listened to any environmentalists, but they feared him . . .

These companies don't care about you, or your kids, or your grandkids. They have zero qualms about burning down the planet for a buck, so why should we have any qualms about burning them down to survive? . . .

"Violence never solved anything" is a statement uttered by cowards and predators.

Talk like this explains why YouTube once banned the use of "Uncle Ted," a nickname often seen online and in graffiti. Reading Kaczynski has been shaking people up for years, from computer pioneers like Bill Joy (who almost lost his faith in technology) to public intellectuals like Paul Kingsnorth (who started to doubt his commitment to nonviolence) to the restless young men who want to start blowing things up as soon as they put the manifesto down.

There's a predictable sequence. Sometimes all at once, from reading, or more gradually just from living in the twenty-first century, the pieces come together, the picture shifts, and everyone else seems to be living in a dreamworld. That's the Kaczynski Moment, Part One: *Why are they talking about binge TV and the latest media outrage when we're turning the goddamn atmosphere into a vast tanker of Zyklon B? Were we all gelded and put into harness without knowing it? Are we trapped in the Matrix for real?*

Then you realize you're sympathizing with a serial killer. That's Part Two, the one that lands the hook. An odd but surprisingly common reaction often follows:

If this is all true, don't I have a responsibility to *do something*?

This is a book about getting to that reaction. It's about Luigi and his kindred spirits. It's about the dark magic in extreme measures. And there's some real darkness ahead, because Kaczynski's ideas have also been taken up by radical right groups that range from neo-Nazis to a growing tribe of "accelerationists" and eco-fascists, who think we should destroy society by speeding it up instead of bringing it down and don't mind throwing in a little race war while they're at it. In the words of Pool Re Solutions, an insurance company that specializes in covering damages from terrorist attacks, "The eco-fascist narrative draws on an eclectic range of sources, though the writings of Theodore Kaczynski are especially prominent . . . This has potentially serious consequences in a context of increasingly serious impacts of climate change going forward."

But here's the crucial detail: Luigi gave the manifesto only four out of five stars. As with many people who read Kaczynski, he bought the analysis but balked at the cure. A long, secretive campaign to send mail bombs to people in science and technology wasn't his style, and Kaczynski's more considered solution was for a brilliant leader like Lenin or Mao to organize a guerrilla force to bring down technological society by crippling vital systems like refineries and power plants. Even for many of Kaczynski's sympathizers, that never seemed like a realistic goal.

So what *would* work?

At the end of the summer, Luigi Mangione caught a plane back to the mainland and disappeared.

CHAPTER 2

DEAR TED

When the news about the shooting broke, my mind went straight to Kaczynski. If he were still alive, I'd be sitting down to write him a letter:

Dear Ted,

Did you see the news about Luigi? What do you think? Is he the one you've been waiting for?

And he would have written back, telling me I'd misunderstood him once again, not that he ever expected anything more from a journalist. He'd have explained why I was wrong, mocked my mistakes, lectured me about the difference between tactics and strategy, asking me to do a favor or two before wrapping his letter up with some version of *Storm the barricades!* and *¡Viva la revolución!* I could imagine most of his arguments, starting with "improving health care is an irrelevant lefty cause that will only make the system function better instead of hastening its collapse."

But Ted was never great at the human side of things. He was one of those rare people who are capable of being motivated by logic alone. Luigi would have been a new argument to try on him, a different take on tactics and maybe strategy, too—Ted was a fan of B. H. Liddell Hart, a renowned twentieth-century military theorist best known for championing out-of-left-field tactics like surprise attacks to throw the enemy off-balance, and less well known as a colleague of my father's. A CIA station chief who kept Liddell Hart's classic *Strategy* on his bookshelf all his life, my dad at one point commanded the U.S. Special Forces in Vietnam. He organized indigenous Montagnards in the mountains as a guerrilla force. He duped a planeload of North Korean spies into landing at the wrong airport. Indirectly and reluctantly, he even participated in a political assassination. I was a feckless hippie, don't get me wrong, but this was the background for my world. In our house, the Great Game and the domino theory were ordinary topics of dinner conversation.

But that didn't have anything to do with Ted. At least, I didn't think so way back in the innocent days of 2004, when I was just a reporter chasing stories and I met a kid named Zach Fredell, who kept talking about him like he was some kind of prophet. The Unabomber story was already eight years old then and I hadn't followed it while it was happening. In my notes, I spelled Ted's last name "Koszinski," that's how little I knew about the guy. But Zach put the name into my head, and as the years passed, another mention of it would drift through my consciousness. I liked Billy Bragg's cover of a song about the Diggers, which got me interested in the Luddites, which led me to a website called the Ludd–Kaczynski Institute of Technology. That kind of thing.

Meanwhile, the magazine I worked for was sending me out

to do stories about current events. I interviewed Craig Venter about his work decoding the human genome. I spent time with some of the guys who invented Siri as they studied ways to make machines talk. I did a story about a scientist from General Electric with an amazing and well-developed project for small, "fourth-generation" nuclear plants that could make clean energy out of nuclear waste. I covered the 2009 UN Climate Change Conference in Copenhagen, when India and China refused to commit to ambitious reduction goals and all the grand hopes fizzled out in a whimper. I covered the 2015 Climate Change Conference in Paris, tagging along after Dr. James Hansen, the scientist famous for first sounding the alarm on rising CO_2 levels back in 1988. After that, I followed him to China for a meeting with the world's top nuclear scientists. I traveled along the Keystone Pipeline from the tar sands of northern Canada to the refineries of Port Arthur, Texas. At that moment, I was working on a story about a dot-com tycoon who was trying to build a brain implant to download skills like martial arts—not Elon Musk, but playing in the same arcade.

Then I met another young man who talked about Kaczynski, but in updated language, calling him Uncle Ted and using expressions like "Tedpilled," which is like taking the red pill from *The Matrix* that opens people's eyes to the real horror behind their virtual reality dreamworld. This was in 2015, more than ten years after I met Zach, but like Zach this new Ted fan was really smart, a serious scholar and a dogged researcher who'd compiled an impressive contact list of Tedpilled revolutionaries around the world. Both of them seemed good-hearted, too, despite their enthusiasm for violence. At least I think so. Anyway, a good story. So I went looking online and found websites with names like Feralculture, the r/tedkaczysnki subreddit and Facebook groups like Anti-Civilization, some attracting more than one hundred thousand followers. I found books like John Zerzan's *Against Civilization,* a 2005 compendium of anti-civ thinking that ranges from Jean-Jacques Rousseau to Ursula K. Le Guin to, yes, the Unabomber. I found a Fox News piece from 2013 called "Was the Unabomber Correct?" by Keith Ablow, the network's resident psychiatrist, who said the Unabomber was in fact "precisely correct in many of his ideas" and even something of a prophet. There was a group down in Mexico called Individualistas Tendiendo a lo Salvaje (ITS), which translates as "Individuals Tending to the Wild." Founded around 2011 by a group of Kaczynski fans who got their start by translating his manifesto into Spanish, ITS took credit for bombs at technology departments of universities and government agencies such as the country's Federal Electricity Commission, along with various shootings and stabbings. There were other groups with similar agendas and florid names, like Conspiracy of the Cells of Fire and Wild Indomitables.

Crazy stuff. Perfect for me. An editor at *Esquire* thought so too. He gave me the go-ahead to research the story, and finally I read *Industrial Society and Its Future.* In its worst moments, it has a chilly superiority that verges on the inhuman, and Kaczynski pounds so hard on leftists that it gets weird, especially when you know his parents had progressive political views. His arguments against modern life didn't resonate with me much either. I like cities. I like theaters and nightclubs. I kept mixing up *Industrial Society and Its Future* with Sigmund Freud's *Civilization and Its Discontents*, and not just because of their similar cadence. Freud was diagnosing neurosis, Ted was trying to cure it and both offered their own versions of a happy unhappy ending. And I didn't buy Ted's argument that art is a dismissible "surrogate activity" either. I think it's essential and primal, something humans have been driven to since we painted deer and horses running across the walls of caves.

But, yeah, the Kaczynski moment happened to me—not all at once, but gradually, over the course of all that reporting, most of which was assigned to me. I am not generally an ideological or political kind of journalist. I like telling stories. Often, they're about obsessive men doing extreme things that border on ideology or politics, but that just seemed like a natural result of looking for good stories. I was primed for Ted's message by the culture around me, by the apocalyptic possibilities hammered into my consciousness year after year with the same growing intensity that brought those two young Uncle Ted fans into my life. When I read his manifesto, lines like this jumped out: "Let us postulate that the computer scientists succeed in developing intelligent machines that can do all things better than human beings can do them," he wrote. "Eventually a stage may be reached at which the decisions necessary to keep the system running will be so complex that human beings will be incapable of making them intelligently. At that stage the machines will be in effective control. People won't be able to turn the machines off, because they will be so dependent on them that turning them off would amount to suicide."

Ted published that in 1995, long before most of us had ever heard of an algorithm.

I already knew how to find prisoners on the Bureau of Prison's new Web-based search tool, Inmate Locator, having used it to get in touch with various prisoners over the years. So I looked up "Theodore John Kaczynski" and got his register number and address at the federal supermax in Florence, Colorado, where he shared a cellblock with Oklahoma City bomber Timothy

McVeigh and Ramzi Yousef, who killed six people with a bomb at the World Trade Center in 1993. In a short letter of introduction, I told Kaczynski I found most of his manifesto convincing. If I had a single criticism, it would be that his argument was too abstract, too mathematically perfect. "I'm still hoping fuzzy logic will save us, that maybe nuclear power can stave off global warming's worst consequences and we can move to the stars and keep working this out," I said. He told me to read his last two books, *Technological Slavery* and *Anti-Tech Revolution: Why and How*. "After you've read them, I invite you to write to me again."

So I read the books and wrote back to him, this time five single-spaced letters of dogged, earnest persuasion. Yes, I admitted, his books anticipated most of the questions I asked in my first letter. He was a long-term thinker and probably not too interested in the day-to-day concerns of a news reporter. But I did find his analysis of the big picture persuasive. There seemed to be no way to stop technology or even to slow it down much, and something with the power to destroy the world could slip out of a lab at any time. I told him about the tech stories I'd been writing. I said I was worried about climate change and asked how he was doing and what he thought of Donald Trump. Maybe he thought Trump was good in a bad way, like some anarchists I heard about who voted for him because Hillary Clinton would have made a much better president. Trump was the candidate most likely to bring down technological society. But I told Ted that reading his writing actually made me look at right-wingers with a little more sympathy—they were trying to hold on to old ways of living, trying to keep their sense of independence and agency. Then Trump arrived as almost a trickster figure, both globalist and nationalist, old-world and hypermodern, authoritarian but also an outlaw. I mentioned a line from Kelefa Sanneh's *New Yorker* story "Intellectuals for Trump": "His reliance on his own intuition is part of what Trumpists love about him, because it frees him from the tyranny of technocracy."

Kaczynski asked me not to write again for a year. With Trump in office, he didn't want to draw attention to himself. They might cut off his mail. But he did want to clear up one misconception. He didn't prefer the right to the left, he just figured leftists were more likely to latch on to the anti-tech idea, and he didn't want any partisan group taking over the revolution. "Since an influx of rightists was unlikely anyway, it was mainly the left I had to drive away."

Before signing off, he added another intriguing statement: "It's certainly an oversimplification to say that the struggle between left & right in America today is a struggle between the neurotics and the sociopaths (left = neurotics, right = sociopaths = criminal types), but there is nevertheless a good deal of truth in that statement."

At the time, this seemed like evidence of a lively mind. Now I see something I didn't see before—how Ted assumed a godlike posture, far above the human fray.

CHAPTER 3

DEAR LUIGI

Now I'm writing to Luigi.

Dear Luigi:

I don't know if you got my first letter. Some of the things
I wrote about might have raised alarms with the prison
guards, especially the references to my long correspondence
with a famous prisoner at the Federal Supermax in
Colorado. But before I get into all that, I want to say this—
I know you're a real person who sacrificed a promising
young life. I saw you plead not guilty at your arraignment.
I heard your voice, I saw your face and that dazed, stony
expression of someone being stared at by the world. That
made all this real. Your attorney touching you on the
shoulder, saying "This is a young man," that made it real.
And you might actually be innocent. The prosecution has
been acting strangely, stalling on discovery while the cops
share some of the materials for an HBO documentary. There

seems to be some question about where the cops found the physical evidence. But if it was you, you pulled your mask down to smile at that hostel clerk. You left the bullet casings saying Deny Defend Depose. You threw away a backpack filled with Monopoly money. So I figure on some level you wanted people like me to tell the tale.

I went on from there, trying to keep it professional, but also being honest about my motives, just like when I wrote to Ted. My set point as a reporter is curious outsider, and usually that's not a problem, but this time I was down there in the cheap seats just like everybody else, mesmerized by the explosion of glee and sympathy that swept the world. I felt it, too, that sudden, almost delirious reversal of values, the dizzying cliff's-edge lurch when "deny delay depose" flew like hail in a digital hurricane and another flurry of messages issued a correction—no, it's deny, delay, *defend*. "Thoughts & prayers," someone said, and a minute later, a thousand people repeated it. Then someone upped the ante: "Thoughts & prayers out of network." Then someone else raised it again: "I'm sorry, prior authorization is required for thoughts and prayers." And when UnitedHealth Group posted an official statement on Facebook, just hours after the shooting, that their "hearts go out to Brian's family and all who were close to him," people replied with so many laughing emojis, a reporter tallied the day's total: Out of 46,000 responses, 41,000 were laughter. "All jokes aside," one commenter finally said, "no one here is the judge of who deserves to live or die. That's the job of the AI algorithm the insurance company designed to maximise profits on your health."

You've indulged in doomscrolling? This was shockscrolling, thrillscrolling, almost crimescrolling. Reading the messages felt illicit, laughing marked you as a co-conspirator. On TikTok, the young woman huddling under a blue blanket: "All of the CEOs out there being like, 'I'm so scared, violence is not the answer,'" she snickered. "Gen Z is really sitting here like, 'Oh my god, y'all really raised the school shooter generation and now you're asking us for sympathy?'" Lawmakers are so callous about violence toward students, she pointed out, they've actually suggested bulletproof backpacks as a solution. "Welcome to a regular Tuesday at school in America."

A mug shot of Brian Thompson with the caption "I killed 400,000 people by denying them needed healthcare," and next to that, Luigi's mug shot: "I shot and killed a guy who killed 400,000 people."

The three options when UnitedHealthcare denies your insurance claim? "Give Up," "Try Again" and "Call Luigi."

The "alibis" meme came in a thousand versions, all very badly photoshopped. "It was great seeing my friend Luigi Mangione in Tulsa on 12-4-2024 between 6am and 6pm." "I had great time with a very good friend of mine named Luigi Mangione and his family from December 3rd (Tuesday) to December 10th (Tuesday) of 2024 at the Taj Mahal. I remember him telling me how much he absolutely hates murdering CEOs and he would never do that . . ."

Was it ghoulish of me—of us—to enjoy this? We're talking about the life of a man, Brian Thompson, the CEO of United-Healthcare, father to two sons. Of course it is. But in situations like this, the ghoulish insensitivity of any commentary has to be discounted by the hyperreality of media events, in which everything is real and nothing is real. Here the border between the two was especially porous. Transgression was the point, humor just the form it took. In New York City on the morning after the shooting, anonymous activists put up signs with CEO mug shots on them. WANTED! DENYING MEDICAL CARE FOR CORPORATE PROFIT. Brian Thompson got his own poster with his face crossed out by an X. In Seattle, someone reprogrammed a couple of electronic highway signs: ONE LESS CEO . . . MANY MORE TO GO. The day after Luigi was arrested, a forty-two-year-old woman named Briana Boston was on the phone with Blue Cross Blue Shield when they denied her claim. Furious, she muttered, "Delay, deny, depose—you people are next." The cops showed up within hours. Boston apologized and said she didn't own any guns but saw no reason to withhold her personal opinion, which was that health insurance companies were evil and "deserved karma." The cops charged her with threats to conduct a mass shooting or incident of terrorism. Her bail was set at one hundred thousand dollars. This was in Ron DeSantis's Florida and the charges were dropped, but still.

Which just inspired more internet anger. "The police won't follow up on domestic violence or death threats but they'll follow up on those three words?"

With stunning speed, the undercurrent of defiance became a flood. People started getting tattoos: DELAY DENY DEPOSE inked over red roses, images of Luigi flashing that smile at the hostel clerk. They sang songs for him on TikTok, made playlists on Spotify, wrote fanfiction on Archive of Our Own. "After committing the perfect crime, Luigi Mangione flees to the Outer Banks to start over, adopting a quiet life as a pool cleaner . . ." Within the week, more than a hundred souvenirs went up for sale on Etsy and eBay, from T-shirts to votive candles, even Christmas ornaments. eBay gave a statement saying that while the platform had a policy prohibiting items that glorified or incited violence, they were allowing the sale of items with the phrase "deny defend depose." When the media connected the inscription on the shell casings to the title of a book by Jay M. Feinman from 2010, *Delay, Deny, Defend: Why Insurance Companies Don't Pay Claims and What You Can Do About It*, every copy on Amazon got snapped up, and the price of used copies on eBay shot to $315.

A story that Anthem Blue Cross Blue Shield was going to put a limit on how long anesthesia would be covered during a surgical procedure suddenly went viral, too, throwing another jolt into the mix. *If the surgeon takes too long, we're on the hook for the drugs that keep us sleeping? Do they wake us up? Are you fucking kidding me?*

Even before Luigi was arrested, a group of about fifteen people calling themselves the December 4th Legal Committee started a fundraiser to help with the unknown shooter's legal bills, setting their target at $500,000. If the person charged with the shooting didn't want the money, they said, they would donate it to "other U.S. political prisoners and defendants facing politicized charges." After Luigi's arrest, contributions took off:

$1000 For my mother. A victim of the insurance industry. RIP. To Mr. Mangione: thank you for your sacrifice. May others follow in your footsteps of bravery and justice.

$100 Thousands of people are put to death for insurance company profits legally each year. How is that system not terrorism?

$50 Luigi Thank you for being a benevolent catalyst for change that we've so desperately needed. You are an angel.

> $10 I've never had so much love in my heart for an inmate
> before!! Beautiful soul!!!

By the end of the first week, the fund raised more than
$110,000.

In my own life, some of my closest friends and loved ones
responded to Luigi with an enthusiasm that startled me. A friend
who teaches middle school in Oregon sent a picture of himself
from the gym, flexing in a *Mario Kart* Luigi T-shirt. The caption:
"Luigi Strong!"

A college buddy who works in a grocery store in upstate New
York said his coworkers were cheering Luigi on and putting up
stickers that said FREE LUIGI! Not everybody in the produce
department, but almost everybody in the meat department—
especially Angel, one of the head negotiators for a fair union con-
tract. "We need more Luigis," she said.

A former investment banker named Ali Flint got in touch,
too. She's as kind a soul as I've ever met, so her reaction really
surprised me: "The day after the shooting was the first time I
understood the phenomenon of cutting. There's so much pain
and powerlessness then bam, a hot guy takes out a CEO in cold
blood, the stockholders walk on the bloodstained sidewalk to get
to the meeting on time, and the press goes to work denouncing
the Americans cheering with relief, the same relief cutting brings."

In her imagination, Ali found a way to participate in the pain.
Her portfolio was Big Pharma in Europe, so she studied all the
health care companies and learned that, basically, the United States
is the global health insurance profit center. Then she helped a few
loved ones through cancer and cancer-related insurance problems.
Throw in the opioid epidemic and the Sacklers—she'd just fin-

ished reading *Empire of Pain*, Patrick Radden Keefe's account of
the billions the Sackler family made off the lie that OxyContin
wasn't addictive—and Ali won't admit to full-on sympathy for
Luigi, just gratitude that the system finally snapped. "Was the
CEO a good guy?" she asked. "Yeah. I've worked in banking,
they're great people. When they say 'thoughts and prayers,' they
actually do mean it. That's part of the cutting."

A pharma banker reading *Empire of Pain*. There's a tension,
then a release.

•

No wonder mainstream publications began to try to tamp down
enthusiasm. They used photographs of Luigi sparingly, told us he
had a "manifesto" but wouldn't print it. Trying not to glamor-
ize killers is standard media practice, but some people found this
suspicious. Here's the muckraking filmmaker Michael Moore:
"On Monday, the mainstream media was breathlessly reporting
about Luigi's 'manifesto.' On Tuesday, though the manifesto was
leaked, the mainstream media refused to publish it. By Wednes-
day, with the whiff of a perfectly choreographed PR move, the
mainstream media stopped calling it a 'manifesto'—now it was 'a
letter' or 'a confession' or 'rantings.'"

In *The Washington Post*, the job of dousing the flames was
given to the former head of Planned Parenthood Dr. Leana Wen:
"The brazen public murder of Brian Thompson, the 50-year-old
UnitedHealthcare CEO who leaves behind a wife and two sons,
should have prompted an outpouring of grief," Wen wrote on
December 12. "Instead, far too many people responded with
glee."

The *Post*'s readers weren't having it.

And what would be the appropriate reaction to the murder of a mob boss?

I am so sick of the media scolding the American people for their feelings about this tragedy. As Luigi shouted: we are more intelligent than you think.

CEOs should be directly and personally liable when their corporation, by policy or by intentional negligent inaction, violates the law in a way that any other "person" would be. No more "corporation pays a big fine" and the CEO gets a bonus for high profits.

In the same paper on the same day, the conservative columnist Megan McArdle dismissed the whole controversy with an airy wave: "What is it about the American health-care system that deranges so many people? I'm not just talking about the man who allegedly murdered UnitedHealthcare CEO Brian Thompson. I'm also concerned about the performative sociopaths" on social media.

The responses noted McArdle's "bewildering" cluelessness about the realities of the health care bureaucracy: "I'm a family physician," one reader wrote. 'Delay, deny, and defend' is not just a slogan, but a widespread strategy to avoid paying for care. Our office spends several hours a day submitting paperwork or talking on the phone to get coverage for our patients."

In *The New York Times*, Bret Stephens took on the gatekeeping job. Luigi was just "Raskolnikov with a silver spoon," he argued. "Angry rich kids jacked up on radical, nihilistic philosophies can cause a lot of harm, not least to the working-class folks whose interests they pretend to champion." A more somber alarm came from University of Chicago professor Robert A. Pape, a longtime scholar of political violence, who thought the shooting could turn out to be "a threshold-breaking attack" that would normalize political violence for young people. He urged political leaders at all levels to condemn violence in general and Luigi in specific, concluding with a sentence that seemed very much like an anguished plea: "The ballot box, not guns, is the right way to settle disputes in America."

Fox News tried to make it a partisan issue, of course. Laura Ingraham said that "liberal wackos are treating suspected killer Luigi Mangione as a folk hero." Sean Hannity accused a Luigi fan of "putting a smiley face on assassination." So reporters went out to gather response quotes from liberals like Elizabeth Warren ("This is a warning that if you push people hard enough, they lose faith in the ability of their government to make change") and Alexandria Ocasio-Cortez ("This is not to say that an act of violence is justified, but I think for anyone who is confused, or shocked or appalled, they need to understand that people interpret and feel and experience denied health insurance claims as an act of violence against them"). In the world of male influencers, the reaction ranged from Joe Rogan's skeptical shrug ("It's like you feel cool saying it," but nobody really wants someone to get assassinated) to Ben Shapiro's furious fifteen-minute defense of traditional social standards in a podcast called "The EVIL Revolutionary Left Cheers Murder!"

Even the radicals at *Jacobin* magazine demurred. "Mangione's murder of Thompson hasn't saved any lives, nor will it; it won't make UnitedHealthcare any less rapacious or lead to the establishment of Medicare for All in the United States. Its only effect has been the death of Thompson."

Then something shifted in the Matrix.

I'm a MAGA Trump supporter who listens to almost every single *Ben Shapiro* episode, but I completely disagree with Ben's bad take and how he is spinning this. He shouldn't be making this about left vs. right. I hope Ben sees the immense backlash and wakes up.

Ben, I really don't care about the left vs right movement anymore and [it's] evident most people here don't. I'd like proper healthcare for my family for once. I'm starting to realize at the end of the day it was never a right vs left battle but the elites vs the common man.

THIS IS NOT LEFT VS RIGHT BEN THIS IS RICH VS POOR

Rogan's fans felt the same:

After listening a bit, I disagree about the Luigi thing. That's not a left vs right issue. It's a class issue. Not that I condone the murder but don't Americans always talk about revolution as a last resort? Hence the Second Amendment? Our leaders aren't giving us many options.

This will continue to happen when money is prioritized over human lives. Sounds like a good time to change the system.

I don't want to skip over all the "drooling," as the *New York Post* put it. Here's a TikToker going by @imanaturalblondeiswear grinning into her camera: "I just sent Luigi a letter does this mean we're going to be together?" Another woman gave a little shiver of excitement: "Honestly, it feels cathartic and sexy to want to do something and then do it—hhnnmmff—I mean writing a letter." Jonathan Van Ness from *Queer Eye* said the show's tenth season should be all Luigi all the time. "I would not touch those gorg curls," he promised. Jimmy Kimmel called Luigi "*Time*'s Sexiest Alleged Murderer of the Year." *Daily Show* correspondent Michael Kosta asked if he was really even hot. "I mean, take away the hair, and the abs, the face, the arms, that easy smile, the way his eyes light up—wait, I'm sorry, what were we talking about? Syria?"

Funny. But these responses also edge up to a disturbing truth: Handsome outlaws are an act of magic. Somehow, their good looks give us permission to celebrate their violation of the rules we follow. Although never quite like this, with such open enthusiasm and T-shirt sales outside the courtroom, not in the America we thought we knew. This was the energy of a culture changing, of old ideas being questioned and new ones gaining traction, of a new consensus gathering. At the Network Contagion Research Institute in New Jersey, a spokesman named Alex Goldenberg issued an alarmed warning. "The dynamic we are observing is eerily similar to the activity on platforms like 4chan, 8chan, Discord, and in other dark corners of the internet, where mass shootings are often met with glee," he said. Luigi's popularity was "a catalyst for the normalisation of political violence that was once confined to extremists on the fringes."

Even a magazine as mainstream as *The American Prospect*, cofounded by Robert Reich, a former U.S. secretary of labor, marked the day of Luigi's arrest by printing an excerpt from a 2019 novella by Cory Doctorow in which a grief-stricken father bombs his daughter's insurance company. "Someone in that building made the decision to kill my little girl," he says, "and every one else went along with it. Not one of them is innocent, and not one of them is afraid. They're going to be afraid, after this." His example inspires a movement called #HeShouldBeAfraid, a series of additional bombings and shootings and, finally, when the bloodshed becomes too much, a universal health care law called Americare. The story ends with a dangerous question: "Who says violence doesn't solve anything?"

And the public rage kept building. On X and Instagram, people posted Bugs Bunny in a tuxedo captioned "I wish all CEOs a healthy fear of the working class." Hashtags like #EatTheRich went viral. "The press is calling me to ask, 'Why are people angry, Mike? Do you condemn murder, Mike?'" Michael Moore said at the end of an epic jeremiad. "Yes, I condemn murder, and that's why I condemn *America's broken, vile, rapacious, bloodthirsty, unethical, immoral health care industry.*"

After nine days of this, the CEO of the UnitedHealth Group tried to wave the white flag in a *Times* opinion piece headlined "The Health Care System Is Flawed. Let's Fix It." This was Andrew Witty, Thompson's boss, UnitedHealthcare (UHC) being a subsidiary of the UnitedHealth Group (UHG), which also owns Optum, which owns Optum Health and Optum Rx, which own lots and lots of medical practices and pharmacies. "No one would design a system like the one we have," he implored. "And no one did. It's a patchwork built over decades. Our mission is to help make it work better."

Times readers couldn't believe his gall.

I'll start listening when Witty's $23 million compensation package is directly linked to patient outcomes.

Perhaps start by prohibiting any lobbying by the insurance or
for-profit healthcare industry, and then we can talk about things
that are in or are not in his control.

Who is he kidding? Insurance companies like his will continue
to deny and delay if it affects the bottom line. His business is all
about profit.

The solution is a single payer system like that which exists in
most advanced countries.

After 2,468 repetitions of these themes with almost none in
Witty's defense, the *Times* turned the comments off.

•

Here's another disturbing truth: Signs of the shooting's impact
came immediately, not just in the huge national conversation
it sparked. Congress announced a couple of bills to force insurers to sell off their "pharmacy benefit managers," another
legal fiction UHC used to wring a few more dollars out of drug
prescriptions. Evan Nardone, the chief technology officer at
St. Moritz Security Services, reported CEOs' requests for security more than doubled overnight, to the sardonic amusement
of many. Two days after Luigi's arrest, Reuters sent out a story
headlined "Health Care Executives Reckon with Patient Outrage
After UnitedHealthCare Killing." Amid the usual denunciations
of murder, Pfizer's "chief sustainability officer" admitted deeper
impacts: "I think all of us are taking a step back and trying
to understand what's happening with patients and their experiences." Anthem Blue Cross Blue Shield scuttled backward so

fast, it changed time zones. "To be clear, it never was and never will be the policy of Anthem Blue Cross Blue Shield to not pay for medically necessary anesthesia services," their sacrificial PR rep said before eviscerating herself on live TV. "The proposed update to the policy was only designed to clarify the appropriateness of anesthesia consistent with well-established clinical guidelines."

Yeah, right.

Reaction stories came out in waves, each explanation edging dangerously close to an endorsement. *ProPublica* ran a piece about UHC's efforts to cut back on childhood autism treatments—just by kicking doctors off their approved list to force parents to find a new doctor, the corporation found it could trim back as much as 19 percent of its autism patients. This despite its having been fined $14.3 million in 2021 for employing similar tactics by illegally denying mental health care to twenty thousand New Yorkers. CNN did a piece about a woman arguing with her insurer on the phone as she was getting chemo for her leukemia. Her copay was $13,000 a month, so she skipped three months of treatment. "It's such a cruel system. We live in a country where people are truly kicked down when they are at their weakest and most vulnerable, both physically and emotionally." *The Washington Post* published "Deny and Delay: The Practices Fueling Anger at U.S. Health Insurers": "Every year, health insurance companies deny tens of millions of patient claims for medical expense reimbursements, and the tide of those denials has been rising." Worst are the preapproval demands, which nine out of ten doctors have said caused treatment delays. In 2024 alone, ten states passed laws trying to cut down on the constantly expanding list of treatments requiring approval. And the news of rapacious profit seeking by UHC kept coming. According to the Senate Permanent Subcommittee on Investigations, the denial rate in the company's Medicare Advantage program went from 8 percent in 2019 to 22.7 percent in 2022. A Federal Trade Commission study showed that over a five-year period ending in 2022, UHC had been overcharging wildly for drugs and treatments that addressed conditions like cancer and HIV. Along with CVS and Cigna, UHC used overcharges like this to bring in a profit of $7.3 billion.

By January, the lines had blurred even more. Pro-Trump influencers like the Wall Street Apes were posting lurid stories on X about bad actors in health insurance: An employee in the UHC claims department said she was taught "thousands" of ways to deny claims; another told of garnishing a widow's wages to pay off her dead husband's pancreatic cancer bills. On more left-leaning social media platforms like Threads and Bluesky, people alternated between their new enthusiasm for non-nonviolence while posting and reposting a meme of one of Luigi's last likes on Goodreads, a quote from Dr. Seuss's classic children's book about an environmental apocalypse, *The Lorax*:

Unless someone like you cares a whole awful lot
Nothing is going to get better. It's not.

On December 17, just two weeks after the shooting, Emerson College released a stunning survey of one thousand registered voters: *41 percent* of eighteen-to-twenty-nine-year-olds thought killing that CEO was "somewhat" or "completely" acceptable.

YouGov conducted a survey with another one thousand people and got similar results. The next day, *Newsweek* published a story saying jury nullification could make it hard to convict the shooter. Former federal prosecutor Neama Rahmani gave the money quote: "I've never seen an alleged murderer receive so much sympathy."

My friend Ali, still on the warpath, followed up with some damning details:

2021—Brian T becomes CEO, UHC implemented the AI that increased the claims denials exponentially. One of the main targets is Medicare recipients near death, cheaper to let them die since they're gonna die anyway. (My words not theirs, obvi.)

2022—UHC explored how to use AI and machine learning to predict which denials would be appealed and which appeals were likely to be overturned.

2023— Class-action lawsuit against UHC for knowingly deploying AI instead of doctors to deny claims under Medicare Advantage; UHC knew the model had a 90% error rate.

The capper came on December 20, when the invisible meme factories of the world crystalized the moment into a single image: Saint Luigi, a strikingly handsome, dark-haired Luigi painted as a medieval icon in holy robes, with a golden halo and a burning heart. The image first arrived in the form of an illustration taped above the cash register at Vito's Pizza, a strip mall restaurant near Luigi's childhood home in Maryland. The owner's daughter put it up to protest the health care system and someone posted a photo to social media. The image went viral, spawning a dozen variations, and soon the owner was getting angry calls and even a death threat—but also tearful stories about struggles with the health care system and offers to buy his customers free pizza. None too happy with the health care system himself, he kept the photo up for weeks.

Online, the reaction was giddy: "WTF I'VE BEEN TO VITOS. ITS MY CHILDHOOD PIZZA PLACE I DIDN'T KNOW IT WAS BASED TOO???" Meaning "based in facts" in Gen Z slang, a way of saying "thumbs-up." But for those alert to the current merging of conspiracy theories with spirituality—of course there's a term for it, *conspirituality*—Luigi's burning heart reframed the shooting as an act of saintly self-sacrifice in the style of "narco-saints" like Jesús Malverde, a Mexican bandit often pictured with a halo and a gun. As one of Luigi's fans put it, "A man risked everything to exact accountability in an era where there's no accountability and this released a torrent of emotion and love."

Even my sister—my seventy-two-year-old sister who walks with a cane and spends whole days drawing Zentangles—felt it, sounding shocked at herself but also exhilarated: "My first reaction was, 'Finally, a good guy with a gun!'"

She can be pretty salty, but this was extreme. I said, "You're kidding, right?"

But no. "I saw these idiots on *The View* say violence is never the answer, just vote," she said. "I've voted always, and nothing changes. That's when violence is the answer."

"How can you *say* that?" I asked.

She didn't hesitate. "CEO salaries—in the seventies, they made thirty times the average worker. Now it's three hundred times. That UnitedHealthcare CEO was fine with denying claims so he could be a millionaire."

If our father could hear her now, he'd probably have to inform a senior officer.

CHAPTER 4

KINDRED SPIRITS

Rod Coronado sank two whaling ships in 1986, when he was just twenty years old. After that, he led a small team into the Michigan State University mink research center, where he firebombed a lab and burned up all their research data, causing more than a million dollars in damages. At Washington State University, where professors funded by the fur industry were researching better ways to raise and trap the future fur coats of America, he and his collaborators cut a hole in the ceiling, smashed all the computer equipment and doused everything in acid. Coronado was twenty-five by then, nearly Luigi's age.

After serving five years in prison, he went right back to the fight, organizing a small group of protesters to harass executives from the redwood-cutting corporation Maxxam. "We're gonna go to your homes every weekend," he said. "We're gonna go to your country clubs, we're gonna go to your favorite restaurants, we're gonna go to your places of work, we're gonna hound you and harass you."

At the time, this was a shocking escalation. To confront CEOs at their homes?

But Rod wasn't the one who worried me. He drew the line at hurting people.

Zach Fredell, I wasn't so sure about. Zach is the one who reminds me of Luigi.

Zach was one of those tall, handsome kids who make rags look glamorous. He was articulate, well read, full of positive energy. His dad was in real estate and doing well, so Zach was another rich kid, too, at least by most people's standards. He was also the first person I'd ever met who had something good to say—who had anything to say—about Ted Kaczynski.

We were in the mountains south of Tucson, getting ready to break the law. Matt, Sprig, Lenny and Diana were the other members of the team, all members of Earth First! in their twenties and thirties. I was following them for a magazine. The year was 2004 and March was just starting, the nights were still cold. Every so often, Rod would send Zach to scout the next bend.

"He always sends Zach up ahead," Matt said.

This was because Zach would bound down the trail like some kind of mad goblin, bouncing over rocks and scurrying up hills, appearing and disappearing on hidden springs.

"I don't hear any shotguns," Matt said.

"They don't use shotguns," Zach said. "They use thirty-ought-six. That's the most-used bullet in the history of man. It's killed more animals and more people than any other bullet."

Lenny rolled his eyes: "The militia of one."

Another time, Zach and Rod were talking about Tre Arrow, a militant activist from Oregon who had been arrested a few weeks earlier. "For stealing bolt cutters," Zach said.

"Fucking hell, that explains it," Rod said. "Before, I thought, dude, he shouldn't have been shoplifting. But if he's doing a job . . ."

"The anarchist's key," Zach said with a knowing nod. Bolt cutters were used to cut through everything from chain-link fences to padlocks, he explained. An essential tool for the serious saboteur.

As we stumbled down yet another rocky wash, he started talking really fast about someone named Ted. "I'm less interested in the anarchist, Luddite kind of anti-technology stuff which I've been hearing all my life than in the critique of the scientific mentality from somebody who was inside it, who was a scientist himself."

It took me a minute to figure out who he was talking about. "But Ted Kaczynski *killed* people," I said.

"All of his hits weren't bad," Zach answered. "The lumber guy, for example, wasn't so bad."

The "lumber guy" was Gilbert Brent Murray, a lobbyist for timber companies. He was forty-seven years old, a father to three children and a Little League coach.

Zach was nineteen.

•

Around the campfire, Rod talked about the history of his tribe, the Pascua Yaqui. An especially tenacious group slaughtered by the thousands because they were living above deposits of silver and gold and didn't want to move, they kept on fighting until the 1930s. Rod's own grandmother slipped across "the imaginary line" just ahead of Mexican troops so sadistic hundreds of Yaquis jumped off cliffs to escape them. That's why hippies at protests drove Rod crazy when they sang their little hippie songs, like that was ever going to solve anything.

Zach was fully on board. "I'm not a hippie. I despise hippies."

No hippie songs?

"Yeah, I don't do that shit. No pansy dancing around, fucking wearing patchouli oil and smoking pot, thinking that they're saving the world. Get a fucking life."

Anarchists were problematic, too, Zach said. "Because their life is their little piece of anarchy, and so they think that they can manifest it within themselves by not participating in the system. But when that cop rolls down your block, you're still hitting the deck. You're still under control."

He wouldn't be sitting in any redwood trees, either. "I'm not gonna put myself up in the middle of a fucking tree where they're definitely gonna come and get me. If I was up there taking a high position with a gun or something, that would make sense."

The others laughed, assuming a joke, but Zach just looked at them stone faced. "Nobody in this country's gonna respect any kind of peaceful movement, because this is a country that's always, always been violent, and everybody here understands violence."

Zach was full of ideas. Quantum physics teaches us that light is energy and all matter is composed of the same general substance and in an active state of interaction, for example. He liked the Beat Generation, the Merry Pranksters, Hunter S. Thompson and Subcomandante Marcos, the Zapatista leader. *On the Genealogy of Morals, The Will to Power*, all the Nietzsche stuff—he was reading that, too. He thought that technological society had created droves of drones, people who think in the same kind of patterns, move in the same patterns, do their jobs from the same hours every day, living out predictable little lives that make them totally miserable. "Depression rates are higher than they ever, ever have been before. They're prescribing lithium to two-year-old kids. Why?"

Rod put in a good word for Amsterdam and the Nordic countries.

"Fuck that," Zach said. "It's socialism."

Zach grew up in Colorado Springs, just an hour's drive from Columbine High School. When he was eleven, he wrote a paper on Amazon deforestation that said the only way to stop it was to raise an army and kill the ranchers. In high school, he got interested in computers, which got him interested in hacking and coding and exposed him to "anti-government and pro-freedom subcultures." The mass shooting down the road went off in 1999, when he was sixteen. He became an antiracist skinhead and sprayed Banksy-inspired stencils on buildings around Colorado Springs. At seventeen, he joined the Libertarian Party and signed on to the Free State Project, a campaign to get Libertarians to move to New Hampshire in numbers large enough to take over the state.

He did have an FBI file, he confessed. But it was a complete mistake: They were looking for someone who committed an arson at a Colorado ski resort, and he just got swept up at a protest.

In 2003, he went to Mexico to try to hook up with the far-left militant group known as the Zapatistas, which turned out to be harder than he anticipated. He ended up in Cancún for the World Trade Organization meetings, where he joined ten thousand protesters from all around the world who came to protest globalization, including thousands of Mexican farmers protesting the free trade agreements that forced them to compete with factory farm corporations from the United States. The protesters occupied a building, deployed the anarchist's key against barricades, marched in the streets and finally—after a Korean farmer put a sign around his neck that said WTO KILLS FARMERS and killed himself with a penknife to his own heart—started throwing paving stones across the barriers at the police, who retaliated with rocks of their own. Zach was in the thick of it, a moment he remembered as pure joy.

"Have you ever done anything that made you feel so fucking alive that it made you bust out of your little reality state for just that second and you realize, *Hey, I don't feel alive driving in my car and going to my job and eating fast food and watching my television. I feel like I'm kind of droning through this movie that I've seen a million different times, and it's always the damned same thing.* But when you smash that TV or go through that storefront or throw a tear gas canister at those police, that's what you've gotta do—you gotta do it all the time!"

After that, Zach moved to Tucson and joined Earth First! As a solid leader with a legendary history of sabotage, Rod Coronado was definitely part of the draw. "And he's not much for all the movement bullshit about non-hierarchical organizing," Zach said. "It's good to see that there's actually people out there that are willing to step up and be leaders."

This was one of the controversies on the activist left at the time: patriarchal forms of leadership versus leaderless resistance. As a hippie-hating Free Stater with way too much knowledge of weaponry, Zach was obviously going to be drawn to the command-and-control side of the argument. But he was also anti-tech, eco radical, and anti-globalist. I'd never met anyone like that before, someone who didn't fit into any known category—someone like Luigi.

•

In the dawn, dark figures huddled over a thin fire as Rod pulled out a map. "We're right here, in zone Thirty-One-A. Here we've got the Four Peaks Wilderness area. There's the Superstition Mountains. They're actually not too far away from us."

Zach came out of his tent with his shirt off, showing off the same Gothic lettering that's on Bradley Nowell's back on Sublime's third album cover, only Zach's said STRUGGLE instead of SUBLIME. Another reason to like the guy.

They were there to disrupt the Arizona Game and Fish Department, which wanted to kill four mountain lions for the crime of living in a canyon where a new suburb had broken ground. It was time to strategize. If they saw a ranger or a lion, they'd try to scare off the lion. But what if the rangers used hounds? Should they try to chase them? Distract them? Rod bought a bottle of lion urine on the internet. Should they spread it all over or mark a path deeper into the mountains? Should they wear masks? Should they wear camouflage?

We stopped at a gas station to pick up a copy of *The Arizona Republic,* which had a column about a lion hunt prominently displayed: "This fight isn't over cats; it's over the West. It has to do with how long it will take before Arizona goes from an untamed and natural place to something that only looks that way. A movie backdrop. A landscape that no longer is Arizona but could play it on TV."

None of this mattered much to me. If it came to causes, I'd go for suffering children over suffering animals, not that I did much for either one. I wrote my stories and paid my taxes and hoped that was enough, even though I knew it wasn't.

Like me, Diana seemed pretty mainstream, maybe still a college student. I asked if she could handle the sentence for trespassing in a closed forest, which was six months in jail.

"Hopefully, it won't come to that," she said. But she brought it up again later. "You never get anywhere unless you're willing to challenge your boundaries."

Challenge your boundaries? To Zach, this stuff didn't even come close. "A lot of people need to do minor direct-action stuff to get their balls up," he said. "You've got to go through stages to reach a certain level. But if you step up to that level, you gotta take up the gun, cause they're coming for you."

Was he serious? I couldn't tell.

"People get killed, everybody's worried about that," he said. "I'm not. I mean, to me, shit's gonna happen. Man has never existed in the state of peace. Peace is a false concept created by domestication."

Technology is the root problem, he said. The comforts of modern life turn us into drones.

I told him about my dad's quadruple bypass, the day I fell in love with modern medicine.

"Do you think he'd have needed that if he was living as an indigenous person?" he said.

"If he was living as an indigenous person, he might have been killed by a bear at fifteen."

"It would be an honorable death," he said.

By that time, I understood that a lot of Zach's ideas were rooted in the Unabomber's Manifesto, which I had never read. I asked Zach to explain the appeal.

"Well, (A) I like Ted's writing," he began. "(B), he has a good critique of scientists. And (C) I like him 'cause he just fucking shut up and got out there and lived in a cabin and hunted and gathered his food and wrote in his notebook and tried to off people that fucking sucked."

I laughed. Zach was such a friendly and cheerful soul, so full of life. He spoke lovingly of his mom and dad. How could he say these things?

He looked me in the eye, his answer unwavering. "I want to see a movement arise where people take out hard targets instead of soft targets."

•

Zach's father showed up unexpectedly just before the Game and Fish rangers went in to hunt, so Zach was sidelined that night. Diana and Sprig were busy too. Rod went in with the crew members he could gather. At the mouth of the canyon, where giant saguaros stood like Easter Island statues, he got out the bottle of lion urine and dabbed ten drops onto a sponge, capping the bottle carefully before dragging the sponge on a string behind him.

At a fence: a No Trespassing sign. In a plastic cover nailed to an end post, a Federal Closure Order. Pass this point and face six months in jail.

Matt went through first, holding up the barbed wire for the rest of us. I wasn't too worried. If I got arrested, I'd probably get probation. War reporters follow troops into battle. The mountains were vast and full of hiding places. What was I going to do, chicken out?

As we walked up the dirt road in the cool desert night, Matt talked about life as a Buddhist trainee and of the redwood campaign he'd done with Twig up in Oregon, three years of hard work to save eight ten-acre parcels around eight endangered tree voles. "Sometimes it seems pretty pointless," he said, "but I couldn't sleep at night if I didn't do something."

In the fall, he was starting his first year as a seventh-grade teacher.

For a few hours, we clambered up and down ridges and deep into wooded hollows as they searched for traps to dismantle. They didn't find a single one. Then a hunter in a staging area on the desert floor looked up and saw us on the ridge. Rod took it calmly. Time to head deep into the woods. He didn't expect the helicopter to lift suddenly off the desert floor. None of us did. *Thokthok-thokthok* it roared, and a minute later it swooped over our heads, banking down the hillside like a chopper from *Apocalypse Now*. Everyone stood frozen.

The helicopter swooped back. "They've spotted us," Rod shouted.

We started running up the path, but the helicopter dipped down, dust flew and— "Jesus Christ, there's a trap! Under your feet!"

Thokthokthokthokthok.

When a dog cringes, this must be what it feels like.

•

The judge let us off with one condition: that Rod stay out of the public eye while awaiting trial. Which seemed like a good idea anyway.

At the Green Fire bookstore in Tucson, under shelves stocked with books on global warming and animal liberation, forty people packed in for a rally. A woman from the Center for Biological Diversity said she'd been getting twenty calls a day about the lions. A woman from the suburb bordering Sabino Canyon said she wasn't afraid of the lions; they were the reason she'd moved there in the first place, to live somewhere that was still wild.

Then Zach got up to give the speech Rod was planning to give before the judge issued his order of silence. He promised the audience at Green Fire that Earth First! would keep going into the canyon to interfere with the lion hunt. They'd try to avoid violence, but the fact was Game and Fish represented the hunting industry and always would. Somehow they had to be made accountable to the people. Because there wasn't enough water, and sprawl was killing the desert, and the mountain lions were coming down out of the mountains because we were forcing them down. And it wasn't just about the lions. "This involves every part of everyone's life," he said. "We need to keep standing up and build a movement, because we've always been on the defensive, and we need to go on the offensive."

He talked for another ten minutes, enthusiasm building. "Destroying snares would definitely be a viable tactic," he told them. "And that encompasses the whole idea of sabotage itself—to *attack the infrastructure!*"

Then he turned to the faces looking up at him. "So, does anybody have any questions?"

•

After a legal fight that lasted another couple of years, Rod spent another eight months in prison, then another year for showing a lecture audience how to construct a Molotov cocktail, then another four months for violating his probation by contacting another activist on Facebook. So two years total. During that period, he announced his resignation from the struggle. The time had come to focus on his wife and son. "Don't ask me how to burn down a building," he said. "Ask me how to grow watermelons or how to explain nature to a child."

That's what happens. People can keep going for only so long.

I got off with a five-hundred-dollar fine and probation. I still didn't care about animal rights.

As for Zach, he spent a few days in the mountains trying to avoid rangers and alert lions, then considered the consequences of another addition to his FBI file and headed down to Mexico, where he ended up volunteering his services to an indigenous tribe called the Huichol—which was wild because one of them stayed in my parents' guesthouse while attending medical school and I spent a week in his stone-walled village high up in the mountains of northern Jalisco when I was the exact same age as Zach. Sheer coincidence, but enough to keep me and Zach in touch. At one point, he tried to convince me to fly down to help the Huichol take on a mining company that was threatening their sacred peyote lands, which I almost did before life made other plans for me.

I'll pick up Zach's story when he gets closer to going full Luigi.

CHAPTER 5

THE ARRAIGNMENT

The Manhattan DA charged Luigi with first- and second-degree murder and also terrorism, which is supposed to be charged for actions "intended to intimidate or coerce a civilian population, influence the policy of a unit of government by intimidation or coercion, or affect the conduct of a unit of government by murder, assassination or kidnapping." The maximum penalty was life without parole.

The feds, led by Attorney General Merrick Garland in the waning days of the Biden administration, also brought a murder charge. The maximum penalty for that was death.

Luigi's arraignment in the state case was two days before Christmas. News reports said the venue was 60 Centre Street, but nobody was there when I arrived except a dozen or so lawyers standing in line, waiting for the doors to open. The NYPD guards just shrugged. Luigi Mangione? Never heard of him. Then a woman approached wearing rainbow-mirrored ski goggles and a scarf wrapped around her face. I was at the top of the steps, so I called down. "You here for Luigi?"

Yes, she said. She thought this was the spot too but as it turned out the real location was a block away at 100 Centre Street, and she wasn't stopping for anything. I tried again. "Why are you here?"

"Why am I here?" she yelled back, half over her shoulder. "Because innocent until proven guilty!"

I followed, asking if she was sympathetic to Luigi's cause.

She stopped and glared. "His cause?"

I mumbled something about insurance and health care.

"Being charged with terrorism is insane," she snapped.

By this time, the search for a more personal motive had covered a lot of territory. Theory number one was the obvious assumption that Luigi had some kind of beef with the health insurance industry. He was twenty-six, the age when you get kicked off your parents' plan. But no, it turned out, he was a rich kid. He went to a fancy boys' school near Baltimore called Gilman where the tuition is almost forty thousand dollars a year. His parents owned a radio station, a country club and nursing homes. He graduated from the University of Pennsylvania, one of America's most exclusive schools. He wasn't even a UHC customer.

Theory number two was back pain: In the days after his arrest, someone dug up Luigi's Reddit account and found complaints that his "spondy went bad," a reference to a painful spinal condition called spondylolisthesis. Then we found out about the surgery on his back in April 2023—and the thing is, it worked. He said he felt great afterward. "At day 8 I was taking zero pain meds and haven't had a bad day since." He shared that good news the following October, more than a year before the shooting.

The rush to pigeonhole him moved on. He was actually "a very recognizable type of young male ideology tourist," one observer said, the kind of person who raves about books like John Brockman's *This Explains Everything: Deep, Beautiful, and Elegant Theories of How the World Works*. Or maybe a member of the Gray Tribe, a tech-bro group of libertarians and atheists? A "new tech centrist" with a taste for spirituality and conspiracy theories?

But all the theories and jokes left out one possibility, perhaps because it was too unnerving to say out loud—that his decision to shoot Brian Thompson was actually a well-considered act of tactical brilliance, a revolutionary spectacle designed to pull the left and the right together against a uniquely unsympathetic enemy. If he'd chosen the CEO of an oil company, only the most radical of crunchy greens would have admitted enthusiasm and only after a full airing of their ethical concerns. But, boy, did he reach across the aisle.

The best clues come from the spiral notebook police said they found when they arrested him. The material was tantalizing but patchy with redactions, leaving much of Luigi's reasoning mysterious. On August 15, 2024, he wrote that he was glad he'd procrastinated because the delay had given him more time to learn about UnitedHealthcare. He followed this with four critical words: "The target is insurance." Police also said that he wrote about the idea of a symbolic takedown and that he cited Kaczynski by name, but they didn't release any direct quotes to back it up.

Another hint appeared in a note Luigi wrote on October 22. "This investor conference is a true windfall . . . What do you do? You wack [*sic*] the CEO at the annual parasitic bean-counter convention. It's targeted, precise, and doesn't risk innocents. Most importantly—the message becomes self-evident."

But the message *wasn't* self-evident. What was the symbolic takedown supposed to achieve? A series of attacks on CEOs? The collapse of technological society? A revolution? A better health care system? Aside from insurance, what other targets did Luigi consider?

Six months passed before the New York state prosecutors put more detail on the record in an eighty-two-page filing with the court. The redaction that came after "This investor conference is a true windfall" turned out to be "It embodies everything wrong with our health system." I'm going to italicize Luigi's reasoning for emphasis:

> *The problem with most revolutionary acts is that the message is lost on normies. For example, Ted K makes some good points on the future of humanity but to make his point he indiscriminately mailbombs innocents. Normies categorize him as an insane serial killer, focus on the acts/atrocities themselves, and dismiss his ideas. And most importantly—by committing indiscriminate atrocities—he becomes a monster, which makes his ideas those of a <u>monster</u>, no matter how true. He crosses the line from revolutionary anarchist to terrorist— the worst thing a person can be.*

Luigi thought about these things pretty deeply, it turns out. And he did consider other targets, including the one Cory Doctorow explored in *Radicalized*.

So you want to rebel against the deadly, greed fueled health insurance cartel. Do you bomb the HQ? No. Bombs=terrorism. Such actions appear the unjustified anger of someone who simply got sick/had bad luck and took their frustrations out on the insurance industry, while recklessly endangering countless employees.

Another possible target was a mysterious person or entity no one has been able to identify: "KMD would've been an unjustified catastrophe that would be perceived as sick, but more importantly unhelpful. Would do nothing to spread awareness/improve people's lives."

•

Up the block at the state supreme court, a soaring gray pile of Germanic granite looming over a narrow street, the guards had no idea where the arraignment was being held. The list of trials on a bulletin board showed only the judge's name, not the defendant's. The guard at the information booth on the second floor had no idea where the arraignment was being held. Finally, a young cop took pity and murmured the location, Part 32, thirteenth floor. I took the elevator. There were two lines up there, reporters on one side and civilians on the other. Guards ushered us into the courtroom when the time came, saying, *Silence your phones. Do not use phones in the courtroom. If you use your phone, you will be asked to leave.*

Finally, Luigi came in escorted by a phalanx of guards, his hands shackled to a chain around his waist, another chain hobbling his feet, on his face a hint of a prep school kid's bored scorn: *None of you know what it's like to be walking here like this, all eyes on me, wondering, greedy, full of opinions.* Or maybe that's a complete distortion prompted by his good looks. Maybe the expression on his face was more like disassociation or even a little fear. But he was wearing that maroon sweater and white-collared shirt, very preppy, almost schoolboy, the same outfit his attorney was wearing. She touched him twice on the shoulder, maternal and quietly indignant, underlining his youth and humanity.

The woman sitting next to me in the last row had a pixie face and straight, center-parted hair. "What brings you here?" I asked.

"Spectacle," she said.

Not the answer I was expecting, but honest. This may be why the guards surrounding Luigi obscured most of the courtroom spectacle, standing between him and the gallery with their beefy tattooed arms crossed like human shields—which was silly because the audience was mostly lawyers, clerks, reporters and women of various ages who had just gone through a metal detector and wand search. Maybe they just didn't want anyone to have the satisfaction of seeing him, especially after all the mockery they got for the ridiculous perp walk they staged for his arrival in New York—Luigi walking down the docks in that orange jumpsuit at the center of a creepy line of men in black with black tactical helmets and pointer fingers stretched theatrically down the barrels of their black assault rifles (a scene straight out of *The Matrix*) with Mayor Eric Adams following a step behind in a pathetically naked attempt to distract the public from his own federal indictment. Nobody thought to offer Luigi a protective vest, as one of his fans pointed out, even though the NYPD cops were wearing them—but really, let's be honest, who would have wanted to take a shot at him?

Shifting for a glimpse between the guards, I saw Luigi duck his head to listen to his lawyer, his shackled hands clasped in his lap, a somber expression on his face. I couldn't hear what she was telling him. Eventually, he looked up and said, "Not guilty," not too loud and not too soft, calm almost to the point of neutral. But again, he also might have been scared. Then he walked out with that same people-are-staring face, with guards ahead of him, guards behind him and guards at his elbows—a last bit of stagecraft for our national drama.

•

Outside and across the street, the line of protesters stood, maybe fifteen or twenty of them tucked neatly behind thirty or forty news cameras and a row of barricades. A scruffy young man stood on a trash can, denouncing the health care system in a loud voice. A young woman stood quietly in the back. Would she talk?

"Depends on who you are," she said.

Just an old writer, I said. Unemployed, used to write for *Esquire*, maybe writing a book.

She shrugged. "Okay. What are your questions?"

"Why'd you come out today?"

"To support class solidarity."

This wasn't what I expected. All the signs and speeches I overheard were about the health care system. I wanted to keep her talking. "So, it's a class war thing to you?"

"Yeah," she said. "It is."

I waited. Nothing. She was watching the courthouse.

I nudged her. "Why isn't it left-right?"

"Because it can't be left-right anymore," she said. "I think that this is a very signifying and unifying event that we haven't seen in many, many years, because I think we all have one thing in common and that's that we're all getting screwed over by wealthy politicians and the CEOs."

And what about the idea that murder is, you know, bad?

"I think when we're being murdered legally by health care CEOs, then it's self-defense, in my opinion."

Her name was Olive. I told her about a story I wrote for *New York* magazine called "Children of Ted," which was about people who believed that technology had turned us all into eunuchs helpless in the face of robotic overlords and climate change, so there was a desperation and a desire to act out and he, Luigi, seemed to fit into that context.

"I would agree with you," she said. "I mean, I don't know what else to say other than I agree with that."

In my entire career as a reporter, which includes an interview with the head of the Peruvian secret police, I don't think I've ever questioned anyone who was as good at shutting up. I tried again to prod her: "And you know what I'm talking about, right?"

"I do know what you're talking about, yeah," she said, and shut up.

She gave me her number, which I would discover really was her number, with her voice on the voicemail recording, but she never returned my calls. After the way she'd answered my questions, I wasn't surprised.

I was saying goodbye when she saw Luigi—not him exactly, but the police cars taking him back to his cell at the Brooklyn Metropolitan Detention Center, where his fellow prisoners included Sean "P. Diddy" Combs and Sam Bankman-Fried. "There he goes," she said. "He just left." And in her voice, there was an unmistakable touch of reverence.

When I got back home, I clicked on the December 4th Legal Committee fundraiser. The amount raised was now over $200,000, and the messages were getting more devotional, like tithing.

$5 My second donation to help keep REVOLUTION alive!

$5 This is my daily donation. BT had a family BUT so did all the people that died because of him and his corrupt corporation # FREE LUIGI

$20 Seventh donation. Let's get this brave boy that 500K.

As I scrolled, my girlfriend, Laurie, was talking to a nurse about her next chemo treatment. We met nine years ago and got engaged about five years later. She was diagnosed in June 2024. Her appointment was just two days away when a nurse at the infusion center called to tell her that her health insurance had been canceled. She should try to get it reupped before she came in, the nurse advised, or they couldn't give her the Neulasta she needed to keep her white blood cell count up after her chemo infusions. One dose of Neulasta costs six thousand dollars. And if the blood count wasn't high enough, they would have to pause the chemo. And, well, the nurse on the phone said, the hospital would probably want that money in hand before giving her the drug.

Laurie was close to tears.

I kept scrolling.

$10 Luigi faced an ethical dilemma called the TROLLEY problem: choosing between saving a larger number of people or sacrificing one person. We actually study this in medicine. Bless his exceedingly bright mind and kind presence as described by all who knew him. 4th time donating.

We were lucky, though. On the third try, Laurie's insurer finally accepted her proof-of-income documents. But the message we took away was clear: We were at the mercy of forces much larger than ourselves.

CHAPTER 6

GAMIFICATION

In the spring of 2024, seven months before the shooting, Luigi paid two hundred dollars to become a founding member of a Substack column written by Gurwinder Bhogal, a British writer who explores the darker parts of online life. The membership included the right to a two-hour video call with Gurwinder (who uses his first name). They spent most of that time talking about an essay he wrote about Ted Kaczynski.

Gurwinder remembered the call later in a thoughtful blog post expressing his utter astonishment at the shooting. Luigi had been so warm and friendly, full of compliments about his writing. He didn't seem mentally or physically unwell in any way. Luigi was in Japan during the call, so Gurwinder asked him how he liked it there. Luigi said he admired the Japanese sense of honor, but so many of the people seemed like docile blanks who just followed the rules—NPCs, or "non-player characters," as internet meme-speak has it, the face-in-the-crowd background fillers in video games. He told Gurwinder a story about running to get some Japanese cops to help a man having a seizure on the sidewalk. When they followed him back, the cops stopped at every red crosswalk signal even when there were no cars coming.

"I quickly realized that agency was a major concern of Mangione's," Gurwinder wrote. That was clear from the three essays Luigi singled out for discussion in the Substack column, all of which described "threats to human autonomy." Luigi said Japan was the future dystopia Gurwinder kept warning about in his essays, especially the *hikikomori*, who spent their whole lives playing video games and watching porn in their bedrooms. For Luigi, "such people had lost control over their lives, becoming mindless slaves to stimuli much like the cops who stopped at red lights even when it made no sense."

This wasn't a problem just in Japan, Luigi told him. People were turning NPC all over the world, "living their lives as a series of reflex reactions rather than consciously choosing their behaviors." Japan was leading the way, but the West was following close behind, pushed by tech companies "intent on mesmerizing us into being servile consumers." He wasn't superior about it, Gurwinder said. On the contrary, Luigi recognized that he was an NPC himself a lot of the time. He condensed his sense of crisis to a chilling line:

"Once we'd surrendered our agency, we'd surrender everything else."

In a video call from London six months after Luigi's arrest, Gurwinder told me he thought Luigi was drawn to him by their shared experiences of working in the tech world. "We both originally believed tech was going to sort of save humanity, that instant information was going to make everyone more enlightened and empathy would travel along social networks and everybody would be better off," he said. "And we both entered tech and we both became disillusioned by that, and we both realized that tech could actually lead to a dystopian world as easily if not more easily."

And finally they converged on Gurwinder's essay on Kaczynski, "Why Everything Is Becoming a Game: All the Better to Control You." Although it centers on an act of violence, the essay starts with an insight from behavioralist B. F. Skinner. When pigeons trained to peck a button for food became conditioned to associate the clicking noise of the dispenser with being fed, Skinner found that they'd keep going at the button even after nothing was left to eat—they'd learned to think of the click itself as a reward.

This gave a University of Michigan zoologist named James V. McConnell a fantastic idea. He'd already adapted Skinner's ideas to create psychiatric programs for prisoners and mental patients when he noticed people playing early video games like *Donkey Kong* and *Pac-Man* for hours. So how about a national plan to use the "addictive mechanics" of video games to program people to be good? "We should reshape our society so that we all would be trained from birth to want to do what society wants us to do," he argued.

This was way back in 1970, Gurwinder pointed out, so it was fair to call McConnell a visionary. With the rise of likes, smiley faces, shopping points, progress bars and employee rankings, his intuition has proved true. We *are* being trained from birth to want to do what society wants us to do. On the plus side, Gurwinder continued, gamification provides "a semblance of order and purpose that may otherwise be lacking in people's lives," especially in an era of turmoil and doubt. You could even look at gamification as an attempt to stop things from getting even more out of control, a kind of social self-soothing.

But Ted Kaczynski was also ahead of his time. In fact, as Gurwinder noted in the essay, his theories "eerily prophesize the capture of society by gamification." First the Industrial Revolution took us off the land and into factories, then we got turned into consumers to buy the things the factories made. We were pigeons pecking at our buttons already, and it was getting worse every day. And McConnell wanted to turbocharge that with the addictive algorithms of video games?

So Ted decided to kill him. The letter bomb he sent cut lasting scars into the bodies of McConnell and his assistant, but they survived. Alas, all that pain was wasted. Nobody got the message Ted was trying to send. He tried to kill a zoologist over computer games?

The way Gurwinder saw this, Ted's actions may have been horrible but his analysis was right. We do live inside our phones, checking our feeds, our email, our instant messages and our dating apps even as study after study shows starkly rising rates of suicide and mental distress, especially among young people—because we're getting the clicks and the likes but no food pellets. We're "looksmaxxing" to get higher scores in gamified beauty contests, but marriage and dating are trending down. We compete on *Pokémon Sleep* for the highest sleep ranking. The Rejuvenation Olympics rate us by how much younger we can make ourselves look.

In his video call with me, Gurwinder said this was actually one of the things they talked about the most. Luigi had become highly suspicious of social media platforms and how "tech companies are essentially abusing power and manipulating people," he said. Gurwinder had also addressed these issues in his essay. The dopamine rush bestowed by our algorithmic overlords "explains why so many young men have lost themselves in video games, and are no longer in employment or relationships," for example. "The false signals they're getting from video game progress, combined with the sexual reward of online porn, are convincing their do-pamine pathways that they're winning in life, even as their minds and futures atrophy."

Another example: A South Korean couple who left their premature baby at home to go to internet cafés and play *Prius*, a game where they raised a virtual baby while the real baby starved to death. This is the problem, Gurwinder said. If your baby is dying, raise a virtual one. If you can't find a girlfriend, get an AI girlfriend. Take the blue pill and eat the steak. And these became what Kaczynski called "self-propagating systems." If competing armies win when they clear enough land to feed more soldiers, then they'll keep on clearing the land until they destroy it. That's what happens to pranksters and daredevils who get themselves injured, arrested and even killed in YouTube stunts. It's the reason the culture wars on X get uglier and uglier and nobody ends up feeling the joy of victory.

This is the future, Gurwinder argued. In a digital society, everything would be gamified. The only solution is to try to choose the right games and play for pleasure, not for a reward. So remember, you're not a pigeon trapped in a cage. You're free. "Even in a world where everything is a game," he wrote, "you don't have to play by other people's rules; you have a wide open world to create your own."

•

The other two Gurwinder articles Luigi liked are revealing, too. The first was called "The Intellectual Obesity Crisis," its topic

information overload, "a cacophony of half-remembered gib-
berish that sidetracks your attention and confuses your senses."
Now we're not consuming information, information is consuming us.

The second was "Why You Are Probably an NPC and What
to Do About It." In it, Gurwinder broke down NPCs into five
categories: conformists, contrarians, disciples, tribalists, and "averagers." Conformists are easily manipulated by "woke liberal
bias" and other enthusiasms of the moment. Contrarians are often
disillusioned conformists who stop believing the official story—in
this camp, he included Joe Rogan, Russell Brand, Tucker Carlson
and conspiracy theorists who think globalist puppet masters are
trying to feminize men so they can create a one-world government. Disciples follow masculine icons like Andrew Tate, Donald
Trump and Elon Musk, which is how you get antivaxxers who
think Musk's brain implants are a good idea. Tribalists are like
culture warriors who think the other side is evil. And averagers
take the center in the hope of avoiding the excesses of right and
left, only to lose themselves in nuance.

We are all one of these five at different times because we just
don't have the bandwidth to think for ourselves all the time, Gurwinder wrote. The only solution was to say "I don't know" or
"maybe" to most things and save your passion for the things that
mattered.

Gurwinder and Luigi spent a lot of time talking about how
Luigi could "become more agentic," Gurwinder said. Luigi also
had concerns about intergenerational trauma and confessed some
secrets, which Gurwinder chose to keep private. In our video call,
he said Luigi mentioned a specific family trauma, but what bear-
ing that trauma may have had on subsequent events Gurwinder

could not say. "Probably not directly, but potentially indirectly."
In response to these concerns, Gurwinder told Luigi about the
Greek Stoics and gave him tips on avoiding distractions and living
deliberately. Luigi seemed to listen intently, asking for clarifica-
tion about terminology at a few points.

At one point, Gurwinder asked Luigi what he would like to
see him write about next. "He said, 'You're great at describing
problems, but I would actually focus on solutions.'" More specifically, Gurwinder told me, Luigi seemed to want solutions based in
science. "He was interested in finding data-oriented solutions to
problems rather than focusing on morality. He didn't believe morality itself was a very good way to solve problems. He believed
that you should look at what is likely to have the largest impact
in the future."

When they got back on the topic of Ted's predictions about
the future, Gurwinder began to feel uncomfortable and took a
pause. Luigi was maybe a little too enthusiastic about Ted's ideas,
he told me. He felt like he had to tell him that yes, he agreed with
Kaczynski about some things, but what the man did was horrible.
He killed people. But Luigi stood firm, responding with the same
nuance he'd used four months earlier in his Goodreads review,
that Ted deserved to be in jail but also to be taken seriously. This
seemed consistent with the note to the FBI that police said they
found in Luigi's possession eight months later, which addressed
the issue of violence directly:

I do apologize for any strife or trauma but it had to be done.
Frankly, these parasites simply had it coming. A reminder:
the US has the #1 most expensive healthcare system in the
world, yet we rank #42 in life expectancy. UHC is the 5th

largest company in the US by market cap, behind only Apple, Google, Walmart. It has grown and grown, but has our life expectancy? No. The reality is these mafiosi have simply gotten too powerful and they continue to abuse our country for immense profit because the American public has allowed them to get away with it.

Oddly enough, however, Gurwinder said they barely talked about health care. Luigi said something about it being expensive in the United States, telling Gurwinder he was lucky to have free health care in England, and Gurwinder told him the downside was that you get what you pay for, and they got bad health care. Luigi just laughed and dropped the subject. Later, when Luigi asked him to start a social club for like-minded people, the subject didn't even come up. "He said, 'I'd love for you to set like a kind of monthly meetup with people who are interested in this, in trying to solve this riddle of tech companies being out of control and how we can try to get people to be more agentic in a world where everything's being automated.'"

In his essay about the video call, Gurwinder said he came away impressed. Luigi seemed like not just a nice guy but an especially nice guy, "polite, thoughtful, curious and kind." But he did seem to feel alienated. He talked about the loneliness of modern life. More than once, he talked about how other people were on a different wavelength. As time passed, however, Gurwinder started to wonder. Maybe Luigi was *too* hopeful. Maybe he was *too* friendly. "He seemed like the perfect human in a way," Gurwinder told me. "It sounds quite strange, but there seemed to be no skeletons in his closet. He wanted to help people. He wanted to improve the world. He just seemed to have no flaws." When they hung up,

Gurwinder wondered if Luigi was trying to hide something, but it was just a passing thought.

The next day was Luigi's twenty-sixth birthday. What he did on that day, no one knows.

Luigi's last post on Reddit arrived on May 25, 2024, a video of dozens of people on a sidewalk in China standing in front of their own cameras and phones to make their own videos. The title was "Streaming Overdose 2024, China." He posted it on a forum centered on Ted Kaczynski.

CHAPTER 7

PEAK HOPE

Paul Kingsnorth had his Kaczynski moment, too. He was another Prince Hal like Luigi and Zach, tall and handsome, soft-spoken, gentle in manner and thoughtful in speech. He also had an elite education—in his case, Oxford and the Royal Grammar School in High Wycombe. He spent fifteen years as an earnest reformer, campaigning against "climate change, deforestation, overfishing, landscape destruction, extinction and all the rest." He was having the greatest success of his career with *Real England*, a book about small shops and family farms that was cited in speeches by the Archbishop of Canterbury and the future prime minister David Cameron.

But by then, he was already losing hope, as he announced in a blog post a few months before the book's release: "I've had it. I'm out."

He got depressed after that, really depressed. "It was like going through the stages of grief," he told me later. "You start off with denial and then you move to anger and eventually you get to acceptance."

But acceptance took years. Kingsnorth told me the story in 2017 over dinner in Concord, Massachusetts, two miles from Walden Pond. First, he published *Uncivilisation: The Dark Mountain Manifesto*. Written with another lapsed idealist named Dougald Hine in elegant and mournful prose, this manifesto opened with a quote attributed to Ralph Waldo Emerson: "The end of the human race will be that it will eventually die of civilization."

This was in the middle of the global economic crash of 2008, which made Emerson's "eventually" seem like way too loose a deadline. "The world's elites are scrabbling frantically to buoy up an economic machine which, for decades, they told us needed little restraint, for restraint would be its undoing," Kingsnorth and Hine wrote. "The machine is stuttering and the engineers are in panic."

The crash was just putting an exclamation mark on the growing gloom, they argued. Young people were making less money, had more debt and worked longer hours than their parents. Few had pensions or savings adequate for the long term. "For all our doubts and discontents, we are still wired to an idea of history in which the future will be an upgraded version of the present." But the doubts kept gnawing away, and with each new doubt the system trembled. One result: "Old gods are rearing their heads, and old answers: revolution, war, ethnic strife."

Luigi was eleven.

The answer *The Dark Mountain Manifesto* proposed was stark: Give up. Embrace the doubt. Stop hoping for a magic cure. Forget the dream of colonizing Mars or creating unlimited clean electricity with fusion power. That kind of thinking is exactly what got us here in the first place. We are not "a rope tied between beast and overman," as Nietzsche put it, the idea the Nazis embraced with such enthusiasm. We are not above nature, but part of it, as the coming collapse will soon remind us. We have to accept the grim reality and "look for new paths and new stories, ones that can lead us through the end of the world as we know it and out the other side."

Kingsnorth and Hine published their manifesto in 2009, the year of the Copenhagen Climate Change Conference. This turned out to be "the year of peak hope" in the environmental movement, as Kingsnorth put it later. People from all over were heading to Denmark to save the world, forty thousand of them applying for slots as official attendees and tens of thousands more to protest. Eminent figures like Lord Nicholas Stern called it the "most important international gathering of our time." President Barack Obama was in office, promising to do something about carbon emissions. The stakes were huge: Poor nations were asking for one hundred billion dollars a year to help them adapt, raising the possibility of expensive new global regulations. No wonder *The Dark Mountain Manifesto* sparked outrage. "There was lots of anger from activists," Kingsnorth told me, "particularly climate activists who saw what we were doing as nihilism and giving up. They said we were doom mongers and we should shut up."

Then reality began its advance on hope. Early on the morning of November 17 at NASA's Goddard Institute for Space Studies, a senior scientist named Gavin Schmidt sat down at his computer and entered his password. It didn't work. He tried a few other accounts and none of them worked either. So he logged in with a restricted master code. A second later, the computer logged him off and locked him out.

Someone was in there, fighting Schmidt in real time. Schmidt sent an emergency message to his Web server: "We are being hacked right now."

When they started the system up again, hours later, Schmidt found a forged Web page with the NASA logo and a link to a website containing thousands of what looked like indiscreet private emails written by leading climatologists. The Manhattan NASA office was the professional home of James Hansen, then the most famous climate scientist on the planet. The hacker was tossing the emails in Hansen's face. In one, a scientist named Phil Jones said he had used a trick to "hide the decline" in temperature in a graph. Another scientist wrote that "we can't account for the lack of warming at the moment and it is a travesty that we can't."

Both emails were talking about specific moments and not the larger problem of climate change, but the hack sparked sheer joy in the right wing. They called it Climategate. "This is not a smoking gun, this is a mushroom cloud!" said Patrick Michaels, a "contrarian" climatologist at the Cato Institute who is one of the 3 percent of climatologists who disagree with the scientific consensus. "The Blue Dress Moment May Have Arrived!" the *National Review*'s Chris Horner declared in a headline. Michelle Malkin issued her snap judgment in a widely syndicated column: "The crimes revealed in the e-mails promise to be the global warming scandal of the century."

The circus master at the center of this furor was a genial, chubby fortyish man named Marc Morano, the executive editor of the leading anti–climate science website, Climate Depot. He got his start as "Our Man in Washington" on *The Rush Limbaugh Show*, wearing a trench coat and a fedora to stalk hotels and event spaces in search of evil liberals. It was all very *Naked Gun*, and Morano had dreams of going the comedy route. Then he heard a politician named Dixy Lee Ray give a speech about how environmentalists were using fear tactics in a sinister plot to expand government power, and the light bulb exploded. He spent a few years doing low-budget exposés before finally hitting the national news with a scoop about James Hansen telling an audience at a scientific conference in San Francisco that we'd have to make rapid reductions in greenhouse gases or face a climate catastrophe—which violated NASA's rules on its scientists' making prescriptive statements in public. Morano's story prompted an order from the Bush administration that henceforth all NASA communications would have to be preapproved by public relations staff. Hansen responded in *The New York Times*. "Communicating with the public seems to be essential because public concern is probably the only thing capable of overcoming the special interests that have obfuscated the topic." For that reason, Hansen said, he would not obey the order.

The administration backed off, and Morano's career went into high gear. Hansen noticed one small but ominous consequence: "I had been using the first line of the NASA mission statement, 'To understand and protect the home planet,' to justify my talks," he said, but when he went back to the NASA website, "the first line of the mission statement was deleted, never to appear again."

•

The Fifteenth Session of the Conference of the Parties to the United Nations Framework Convention on Climate Change began on December 7, 2009. I was there, attending my first climate conference, still blissfully clueless about Kingsnorth and Kaczynski. Hope was definitely the theme. The signs on the bus stops all read HOPENHAGEN. There were ads everywhere saying COKE IS HOPE, which had something to do with a corporate greening initiative. I was feeling pretty optimistic myself, having just spent a week with an idealistic, good-hearted scientist working at General

Electric–Hitachi on something new called fourth-generation nuclear power, a technology that was surprisingly far along and
could give the world carbon-free energy by burning old nuclear
waste. If 97 percent of climate scientists were right and we were
truly facing an existential crisis, a conclusion I had no expertise
or inclination to dispute, the old anti-nuke environmentalism was
a category error.

In Copenhagen I spent the week tagging after Morano, which
gave me a glimpse of the war Kingsnorth spent fifteen years of
his life waging, and why he had given up. Morano showed up
at his first event boisterous and jolly, with a five-o'clock shadow
like Barney Rubble's. "Lost my luggage," he explained, shaking hands around the room. About thirty suspiciously clean-cut
college kids were already there chatting up a handful of nerdy-
looking older men who turned out to be pillars of—I don't know
what to call them. They don't like "deniers," but you can't call
them skeptics.

The best known was Steven Milloy, who'd gotten his start
disputing the link between cigarettes and cancer on behalf of tobacco companies. *Green Hell: How Environmentalists Plan to
Control Your Life and What You Can Do to Stop Them* was one
of his books, and he edited a website called JunkScience.com that
targeted government regulators who "use junk science to expand
their regulatory authority" and scientists who "use junk science
to achieve fame and fortune." Milloy was a youthful guy with
a bulldog chest, an air of permanent irony and a grating laugh.
"You can't say you're a socialist, but you can say you're an environmentalist," he cackled. "It's too bad Joe Stalin missed this
one. Hahahaha."

Morano took the podium, surrounded by larger-than-life portraits of Ronald Reagan that covered the walls. "This is a great week to be here in Copenhagen," he said, beaming as he triggered his first slide: "Copenhagen climate change talks must fail."

"Let's play a little game. Who said this? Was it Sarah Palin? Was it Senator Inhofe?"

A familiar voice called out: "James Hansen, hahahahaha."

"James Hansen!" Morano agreed. "*James Hansen* said this conference must fail! So, if anyone asks you this week 'How can you be against this?' say 'We stand in solidarity, shoulder to shoulder, with NASA's James Hansen!'"

He grinned impishly and kept the slides coming: "Al Gore: 'U.S. Climate bill will help bring about "global governance."'"

"This isn't about science," he said. "It's about controlling humans."

If people had time to dig into these accusations, they would have found them grotesquely dishonest. What James Hansen actually said was that if world leaders were going to continue business as usual, the climate talks *might as well fail*. And that Al Gore quote about "global governance"? Gore was just calling for international cooperation. But who had time? And wasn't Morano sort of kidding? Like when he used the righteousness of progressives to mock them? Al Gore used more electricity in a week than 28 million Ugandans used in a year! How could white, wealthy Westerners tell 1.6 billion people of color how to manage their economy? It's a new form of colonialism!

In the days that followed, Morano and his little troupe of climate trolls fanned out in search of fresh targets. During the first big protest march, with more than sixty thousand people banging drums and waving signs that read THERE IS NO PLANET B milling past, a news crew from Sky TV documented a debate between

Morano and a climatologist from the University of London. Morano led with the Hansen "quote" about wanting the talks to fail.

"The nerve of quoting James Hansen," the climatologist sputtered in outrage.

Morano moved on to his next talking point: that sea levels weren't really rising "according to the Royal Netherlands Meteorological Institute."

"Absolute rubbish," the climatologist snapped.

Actually, the report Morano cited said that sea levels had risen almost eight inches over the last century, but he just moved on. He had what he wanted, the clip of the stuffy university professor getting flustered, which he would edit to his liking. A few hours later, he got his first repost on a friendly blog: "Marc Morano Destroys Fake Environmentalist."

Next stop, the convention center, where members of the media were hanging out in a room the size of a football field while the delegates lined up at the registration booths. Milloy mocked them in a loud voice. "This is the way to global socialism. It's not health care. It's not fucking up Afghanistan. It's this—hahahahaha."

Outside, protesters kept marching by—an endless stream of giant puppets and snorkels and signs demanding CLIMATE JUSTICE NOW! One of the Morano kids pointed down the street, excited. "Here come the anarchists!" She watched with wide eyes as they passed carrying signs that read FUCK GREEN CAPITALISM, WE WANT COMMUNISM.

A ripple of satisfaction ran through the group. "You can't be any clearer than that," said one.

But the sheer size of the crowds seemed to irk Milloy. God sure must have loved idiots, he said, because he'd made so many. He returned to the topic again and again. "They may have all these people, and they may have all the signs, but I've got fifty-nine senators, and that's all that matters. They can come here and burn Copenhagen down; it doesn't really matter."

As it turned out, he was right. The "Climategate" story dominated the global headlines the entire week, giving cover to those fifty-nine senators and the forces they represented. Even with Democratic majorities in the House and Senate and President Obama in office, the United States wouldn't agree to any cuts unless China did too. The conference ended without any agreement at all.

•

Watching from the sidelines, Kingsnorth felt sympathy and sorrow. He had a lot of friends at the conference, "people who were desperate to believe something would happen," and many of them sank into their own depressions when they returned home. "You have to be careful about hope," he told me later. "If that hope is based on an unrealistic foundation, it just crumbles, and then you end up with people who are despairing. I saw that in Copenhagen—there was a lot of despair and giving up after that."

On the plus side, *The Dark Mountain Manifesto* caught fire. Thousands of people wrote fan letters, confessing their own lost hope. They wrote songs and plays and PhD dissertations. They started local Dark Mountain groups and went to Dark Mountain festivals. Kingsnorth and Hine started publishing annual Dark Mountain anthologies, big beautiful books filled with sorrow and nature mysticism.

Alas, Kingsnorth's journey to acceptance hit a roadblock. He pinpointed the moment in a startling essay called "Dark Ecology," written just three years after he and Hine published their manifesto: "I've recently been reading the collected writings of Theodore Kaczynski. I'm worried that it may change my life . . . not just in the ways I've already changed it (getting rid of my telly, not owning a credit card, avoiding smartphones and e-readers and sat-navs, growing at least some of my own food, learning practical skills, fleeing the city, etc.) but properly, deeply."

Like Zach, Kingsnorth said he'd heard versions of Ted's arguments before, many times. But there was something about his clarity, his refusal to hedge or to take refuge in nuance: Ted was "logical and unsentimental," pretty much what you'd expect from a former mathematics professor with a Harvard degree. Even worse, his ruthless clarity led the reader step by step to an end without an exit and just left him there, wondering what the hell to do.

If Ted's attacks on artificial intelligence and computer science rattled Luigi, imagine what his attacks on left-wing reformists did to someone like Kingsnorth, who distilled Ted's critique down to a single line: "The political left is technological society's first line of defense against revolution."

The first line of *defense*? What a disappointment! All those years when Kingsnorth thought he was battling the systems of destruction, he was really just smoothing out their harsher edges. He'd served as living evidence that somebody was on the job of worrying about the environment. That was his function in the system. He helped the public sleep easy. Which meant he'd been fighting on the wrong side all along. After all, look at the situation. Use those icy Unabomber eyes. E. F. Schumacher, Leopold Kohr, Neil Postman, Jacques Ellul, Lewis Mumford, Kirkpatrick Sale, Jerry Mander and Edward Goldsmith are just a few of the prophets who tried to warn us, but Margaret Thatcher and

Ronald Reagan offered cheap oil instead. Three decades and one global economic crash later and the system was starting to teeter again. Just look at the UN's 2012 Climate Change Conference down in Rio, Kingsnorth said. "It was accompanied by the usual shrill demands for optimism and hope, but there was no disguising the hollowness of the exercise. Every environmental problem identified at the original Earth Summit has gotten worse in the intervening twenty years, often very much worse, and there is no sign of this changing."

Ted was right about the left, Kingsnorth decided. Just look at the "neo-environmentalists" who were starting to emerge from right-wing think tanks like the Cato Institute, or even more traditionally left-wing groups like the Nature Conservancy. Like the accelerationists, they found an answer in scientific progress. Geo-engineering will cool the planet! Biotechnology will give us carbon-free food! Modern nuclear plants will give us clean energy!

This one lands close to home, given that I am open to all those things, not that they fill me with joy. Kingsnorth calls them progress traps: The perfection of hunting killed so many animals that humans had to turn to agriculture, which led to overpopulation. Pesticides and herbicides saved a billion lives during the Green Revolution, but then we had to come up with genetically modified crops to save them again. Each time we get caught in one of these progress traps, there's no going back, so we just keep making the system bigger and the resulting crash more destructive. "I am beginning to think that the neo-environmentalists may leave a deliciously ironic legacy," Kingsnorth wrote. "Proving the Unabomber right."

But again, there's that nagging question of what to do. "Is it possible to read the words of someone like Theodore Kaczynski and be convinced by the case he makes, even as you reject what he did with the knowledge?"

Here, Kingsnorth came to an uneasy pause. He'd already ditched his modern conveniences and moved to the Irish countryside, just as Ted did when he moved to his cabin in Montana. "I'm not sure I know the answer," he wrote, and left the question there. When I caught up with him a few years later, Kingsnorth was growing his own food and replacing a flush toilet with a composting toilet, not to save the world but just to feel comfortable in his own conscience. "The political model is out of date," he told me. "People power, marching in the streets—it won't work. We all love the fruits of what we're given, the cars and the computers and the iPhones. What politician is going to sell people a future when they can't update their iPhones ever?"

At the heart of the Dark Ecology essay, Kingsnorth put the pivotal moment when all the chain saws and cars and barking dogs finally drove Kaczynski to a breaking point and he hiked up into the mountains to a high plateau that always soothed his spirit, only to find a new road cut right through the middle of it. "You just can't imagine how upset I was," Kaczynski remembered later. "It was from that point on I decided that, rather than trying to acquire further wilderness skills, I would work on getting back at the system. Revenge."

Reading that, Kingsnorth felt the shock of recognition. He could identify, he said, even with the last word.

CHAPTER 8

SUCH RUTHLESS HONESTY

In his spiral notebook, Luigi considered the methods Kaczynski used. But a bomb could "kill innocents," he wrote.

The decision to use a gun would have exposed him to a higher level of danger. He would have had to wait until Thompson walked by and then step out onto the sidewalk where anyone could see him. It was like the note police said they found on him saying he'd done it alone, like the Monopoly money in his backpack, maybe even the Citi Bike he rode to Central Park: He was constructing a puzzle for others to solve. Sending a message.

Another strange detail—he put his review of the Unabomber Manifesto on Goodreads on January 23, 2024, even though he'd read the manifesto two years earlier, in the book club. He posted his review of *What's Our Problem?* on the same day.

The more I dig into Luigi's reading list, the more I see what he was trying to do. It all fits a pattern. He wanted to rise above political categories. He wanted to understand the sweep of historical forces. He wanted to take the red pill and see the green letters fall down the screen.

That's the promise of Urban's *What's Our Problem?* The subtitle spells out its grandly modest goal: *A Self-Help Book for Societies.* And boy, does it give a lot of self-help, 746 pages, which makes sense given its mission of preventing a global apocalypse with nothing but logic, cheerful jokes and cute illustrations. "Our responsibility is immense," Urban writes. "If we can figure out how to get page 1,001 right, Future Us and trillions of our descendants could live high up on that mountain in what would seem like a magical utopia to Today Us. If we get page 1,001 wrong and stumble off those steep cliffs, this might be the last page of the story."

Urban's book is 100 percent laser-focused on the current political crisis in America. Look past our partisan divides, he instructs, and think of politics as a ladder. The lower rungs of the ladder are rooted in the "primitive mind" of tribalism, while the higher rungs are more rational and scientific, aware of the dangers of confirmation bias and comfortable playing devil's advocate. President Reagan was high-rung because he was pragmatic while appealing to principles like patriotism and national unity. He "turned the conservative platform into a beautiful story about freedom and American idealism." He was the big-tent guy who asked, "How can we love our country and not love our countrymen?"

In contrast, Newt Gingrich was "a wizard at the dark art of low-rung politics," appealing to emotions like hate and fear. He taught politicians to use words like *radical, traitor* and *socialist* to describe ordinary liberal Democrats, and the GOP steadily stepped down the ladder to the lowest rungs. By the time Barack Obama came along, "Republican tribalism had become the party's most sacred value. What mattered most was Republican victory in a war against the Democratic enemy, even if that victory had to come at the expense of nearly every core value Reagan had preached."

This is the story of America as most liberals see it, Urban says. But what about the low-rung left? This is where his thinking gets more interesting, especially as it relates to Luigi and Uncle Ted.

To Urban, the arrival of wokeness—he calls it "social justice fundamentalism"—was one of the last decade's defining stories. Starting in 2014, ideas about systemic oppression that had been percolating away in academia since the 1990s started to emerge into the larger world. "White privilege" became a thing. "Believe women" went from general caution to blanket command. Movements like #MeToo and Black Lives Matter led to noxious forms of public shaming that alienated ordinary Americans. As Urban puts it: "Accusations of cultural appropriation have attempted to restrict everything from 'culinary bigotry' in Oberlin's dining hall to white bands playing afrobeat music at Hampshire College to white girls wearing hoop earrings at Pitzer College."

In the spring of 2017, when Luigi was a freshman at Penn, students at Evergreen College decided to flip their annual Day of Absence, a campus event when people from racial minority groups voluntarily stayed home to show how much they contributed, asking that whites stay home instead so the minorities could have the campus to themselves. When one professor objected, saying there was a difference between volunteering and being asked to stay home, angry students mobbed his classroom, called him a white supremacist and demanded his resignation, barricading the door to an administration building. The professor, who had been there fourteen years, wound up resigning.

You can see the whole thing on YouTube under the header "The Evergreen Equity Council," and it definitely seems like a Red

Guard moment. But Evergreen is as lefty as left gets. Also, the professor sued and got a six-figure settlement. What does it all prove?

Urban has a larger purpose. He wants to build a case against the left wing strong enough to make a red pill.

Between 2015 and 2022, he says, student protests stopped one hundred people from giving speeches, some as mainstream as Supreme Court Chief Justice John Roberts and former Secretary of State Condoleezza Rice. Harvard students protested just because *The Harvard Crimson* said it couldn't reach ICE for comment on an immigration story, perhaps distressing undocumented people who couldn't bear to hear mention of the U.S. Immigration and Customs Enforcement agency. Influential books like Robin DiAngelo's *White Fragility* taught white women that "over-smiling allows white people to mask an anti-Blackness that is foundational to our very existence as white."

During all this, social media emerged with a powerful new tool for public shaming. Enter "cancel culture." Urban goes into prominent cases like Donald McNeil Jr. and James Bennet of *The New York Times* and Alexi McCammond of *Teen Vogue*, all forced out of their jobs for dubious reasons. He covers the story of Larry Summers, the former treasury secretary and president of Harvard, who was widely condemned for what Urban considers some unremarkable comments about the rates of women in STEM programs, which led to Summers's resignation. Urban writes about a book called *Irreversible Damage: The Transgender Craze Seducing Our Daughters,* written by a psychologist named Abigail Shrier, who blames the growth in trans identification on social contagion. Despite good sales and reviews, Amazon stopped allowing ads for the book, and the American Booksellers Association, one of the sponsors of Banned Books Week, apologized for including copies of it in shipments to bookstores: "This is a serious, violent incident that goes against ABA's ends policies, values, and everything we believe and support. It is inexcusable."

A violent incident? This reflects another escalation, the idea that speech can be violence. In a 2020 article in the *Journal of the American Heart Association*, a prominent cardiologist crunched numbers to show that affirmative action initiatives in his field hadn't improved patient outcomes. After a furor, the journal retracted the story and the cardiologist was forced to step down from his position as a program director at the University of Pittsburgh, which "prohibited him from making contact with any students," Urban writes, "telling him that any classroom he participated in was 'inherently unsafe.'"

Luigi was in the thick of all this. Trump was elected during his freshman year, when the Andrea Mitchell Center for the Study of Democracy at UPenn held a series of public lectures on gender, race and masculinity. During his junior year, the center's theme was Democracy in Trouble?, with lectures on some of his favorite topics. "Why Do Democracies Fail?" "Why Is Authoritarianism Suddenly Appealing?" "Is Democracy Worth Saving?" "Is Economic Inequality Destroying Democracy?" "How Should Citizens Resist Authoritarian Rule?"

And 2020—well, that miserable year started out with this announcement from the university: *We are writing to share information about the new strain of coronavirus that has been making the news . . .*

•

The way Urban tells the story, Luigi graduated into working life just as social justice fundamentalism was spreading from the universities to the professional world. Companies like CVS and American Express started putting employees through diversity training that became more and more intrusive, including a checklist that asked workers to reflect on privilege and unconscious bias. At the Treasury and the Federal Reserve, employees were told not to "perpetuate white silence" by failing to use terms like "white supremacy." When the Covid-19 vaccine became available in 2020, the Centers for Disease Control and Prevention suggested vaccinating essential workers ahead of the elderly to "promote justice" and "mitigate health inequities," even though old people died in much higher numbers. A UPenn professor defended this idea to *The New York Times*, saying older people tend to be whiter because society is "structured in a way that enables them to live longer," so vaccinating them first would only perpetuate white privilege. Then came the differing responses to religious gatherings and the Black Lives Matter protests, when actual doctors said things like, "In this moment the public health risks of not protesting to demand an end to systemic racism greatly exceed the harms of the virus."

Urban presents a long list of headlines that highlight the trend, briefly excerpted here:

Politico: "The Racist History of Tipping" (2019)

Vox: "The Knitting Community Is Reckoning with Racism" (2019)

Global News: "Dr. Seuss Books Are 'Racist,' New Study Says. Should Kids Still Read Them?" (2019)

The Telegraph: "From Elvis Presley to Patti Smith and the Stones, Rock Music Is Built on Racism" (2020)

New York Post: "Why Your Swipes on Hinge and OkCupid Might Be Racist" (2021)

Book and Film Globe: "Is 'The Muppet Show' Racist?" (2021)

Newsweek: "San Francisco School Board Commissioner Calls Merit-Based Education 'Racist,' Sparking Debate" (2021)

Urban may exaggerate the impact of all this—according to a recent Pew poll, only 21 percent of American workers think DEI programs at work are a bad thing—but he has another goal in mind. He wants to show how low-rung thinking on the right creates low-rung thinking on the left, which creates even lower-rung thinking on the right and on down the dizzying doom spiral. Fox News got a million stories out of woke. State governments all across the country started passing laws against teaching critical race theory. Book bans took off. Then Donald Trump won the 2024 election and threw everything into hyperdrive.

Not Luigi, though. Here's something he posted on X in the summer of 2024: "Both parties—Trump with his refusal to accept the results of an election, and Biden with his refusal to accept his age and step down—are simultaneously proving how desperately individuals will cling to power." He was determined to follow Urban's advice and stay on the high rungs.

But what should come next? That's the tricky part, Urban says. Consider the insanely rapid pace of technology, especially instant, overnight, world-changing technologies like AI. "In the chaos of exponential progress, our societies are beginning to lose their grip," he warns. He even admits that sometimes he feels hopeless himself. But the only way to avoid imminent and certain disaster is to wake up out of fundamentalist low-rung thinking of all kinds, both right and left. We need to see through the falling green letters of our tribal codes and escape them to become "part of the immune system instead of enabling the virus." This may require courage, Urban says, but hard times make strong men. "If you want to be a full hero and throw your career away going down in flames, all power to you."

In short—who can break the spell and save the world?

•

First off, let me just say how curious and impressive it is that Luigi even bothered to read this kind of thing, much less find so much meaning in it. How many young men take on such a sense of personal responsibility for the future of the human race? But of those who do—and it does seem to be a growing cohort—how many think Tim Urban's cheerful, can-do analysis is one of the "most important" breakdowns of our dilemma? And of those, how many would give four stars to the Unabomber Manifesto? The contrast between the two is jarring.

But let's consider some of the ways Kaczynski's and Urban's manifestos overlap. You have to look for it, but Ted did say that most people on the political left, "perhaps even a numerical majority," were decent and fair-minded. He expressed regret about the horrors women were likely to suffer when civilization collapsed. In one letter he sent me, he said he probably would have voted for Hillary Clinton. But he opened and closed *Industrial Society and Its Future* with furious attacks on leftists. As he detailed in sections 7 through 32, whether you're talking about feminists or socialists or disability activists, leftists are "over-socialized" people who have learned to be ashamed of natural impulses like anger and lust. Therefore, they suffer from depression and low self-esteem. They have the nervous tics of caged animals. That's why they identify with outsiders and people with problems, why they like depressing art, why they're suspicious of competition. Section 15: "Leftists tend to hate anything that has an image of being strong, good and successful. They hate America, they hate Western civilization, they hate white males, they hate rationality."

They hate Western civilization? Quite the criticism coming from someone who wanted to destroy it, though this is probably just an early example of trolling the libs.

Ted explained his real reasoning in sections 213 to 230, which make up a chapter called "The Danger of Leftism." Over-socialized people are so bound by conventional morality, the only way for them to feel free is by imposing their morality on everyone (section 221). That's why they can't stop trying to take control of every facet of life. "It's not enough that the public should be informed about the hazards of smoking; a warning has to be stamped on every package of cigarettes. Then cigarette advertising has to be restricted if not banned. The activists will never be satisfied until tobacco is outlawed." This is due to "the quasi-religious character of leftism; everything contrary to leftist beliefs represents Sin" (section 219).

If this sounds very much like social justice fundamentalism, it's no accident.

But Ted went further. The real problem was that leftists didn't rebel *enough*. This was the argument that rattled Kingsnorth so much, that leftists couldn't rebel on a fundamental level because all they really wanted was to make the system better. Not only that, but their overwrought support of conventional norms like equal rights was rooted in awareness of their own servility, which explained their streak of masochism. Their idea of fighting was lying down in front of a bulldozer—useless in a revolution.

Worse, their pacifism discouraged the real radicals from taking action.

The Black Panthers were active when Ted was teaching at Berkeley. The Weathermen were beginning to organize. Ted knew about nineteenth-century anarchists like Alexander Berkman, who spent fourteen years in prison for trying to kill a robber baron named Henry Clay Frick. But they were all too moderate for Ted, too attached to social progress. He was looking for someone rational enough to see that the real enemy was technology itself.

After Luigi's arrest, Urban did a mournful interview with *The New York Times*. "If I imagine the Venn diagram circles of 'people who not only like my stuff but evangelize about it' and 'those who not just support political assassination but do it themselves,'" he said, Luigi "might be the only person in the overlap." How could such a high-rung rational thinker do such a low-rung tribal thing?

But if we take Luigi seriously, the *Times* reporter responded, maybe he decided the system was broken and couldn't be fixed through normal means. So he made a rational choice to commit a high-rung act of violence.

"That is a radical position that I don't agree with and I don't think history supports," Urban answered.

Yes, he could see how someone would read the book and think they "had a special ability to see the world with clarity." But that had to be the result of some kind of mental breakdown.

Except, there were no *signs* of breakdown, the reporter pointed out. No old friends saying how troubled Luigi had been. No one who said he was angry. He disappeared, but in such a professional way, with no loose ends.

Urban couldn't explain it. The idea that somebody got murder out of his book upset him. Violence requires dehumanizing your enemies. Isn't it obvious that if you're okay with killing a health care CEO, somebody will think it's okay to kill the head of Planned Parenthood?

But there was one odd detail, Urban said, an email Luigi sent him in January 2024. He said he'd been reading Urban's blog since he was in high school and there was one line he really liked, the most poignant line he'd ever read there, which he quoted from memory: "A high-level thinker sees a foggy world through clear eyes, while a low-level thinker sees a clear world through foggy eyes." Urban quibbled with the paraphrase. He was really saying that a clear-eyed person sees how complex life is, and you don't kill people if you allow yourself to see their full humanity. But he skipped over Luigi's use of the word *poignant*, which means "arousing deep emotion, especially of pity or sorrow." He couldn't imagine the possibility that Luigi understood just how grave and terrible killing Thompson would be, and decided to do it anyway.

CHAPTER 9

PSYCHOLOGICAL ISSUES

The clock ticked down after Luigi posted his twin reviews. He went dark in July, soon after he got back from his travels in Asia.

His mom reported him missing on November 18, sixteen days before the shooting. She reported him missing in San Francisco because she thought that's where he lived. When the police questioned her about the shooting, she said she could see Luigi doing something like that—at least that's what NYPD Chief of Detectives Joseph Kenny told the media. Yet even months later, nothing turned up to suggest that his childhood was anything but encouraging. He grew up in a big brick house in the suburbs of Baltimore, had two older sisters and lots of cousins, went to Catholic schools till sixth grade and switched to Gilman because he was a brainiac science geek who seemed destined for greatness. He taught himself how to program in ninth and tenth grade because he wanted to make video games. He volunteered as a writing coach. His teachers remembered him for his "humility, kindness and affability," said *The Washington Post*. One example was the way he singled out the accomplishments of other students in his valedictorian's speech. A friend from his robot-making club told about the time their robot fritzed out before a competition and Luigi invited everyone over to his house to eat pizza and brainstorm. He was "always keeping everybody's energy up," the friend said.

He did have a contrarian streak, which he expressed in one of his longer Reddit posts:

> I remember one time as a young child playing with friends. Fantasizing, we each sketched our ideal "dream home." Everyone else drew intricate mansions, complete with elaborate swimming pools and multi-car garages. I sketched the floor plan of a small square house, with four identically-sized square rooms: a bedroom, a living room, a kitchen/dining room, and a bathroom/laundry room. A place to sleep, a place to be, a place to eat, and a place to . . . uh . . . excrete. It was everything I needed, nothing more, nothing less. They thought I was weird. I thought their mansions were full of lots of bullshit.

He let out the tiniest glimpse of a darker side in his Goodreads review of *The 4-Hour Workweek*, by Tim Ferriss. The book was full of fluff, he said, but he loved it because of how Ferriss refused to accept the way things were. Luigi had always been like that too, he said. When he was a little kid, he'd hold his knife in his left hand and his fork in his right, which would "infuriate" his mother. She wanted him to cut with his right hand and then eat with the same hand, which meant switching hands each time. He'd ask why, and she'd say "because that's how to cut." He'd ask why again, and she'd tell him because it was proper manners. "As a six-year old," he wrote,

I found this to be the most pointless and inefficient process
in the world, and I'd voice this opinion. Why would I switch
hands *every single bite* to maintain some arbitrary convention?
The final reply: "One day you're going to meet a nice girl, and
when you go out to dinner with her you'll need to use proper
manners." My response then, and still a fundamental belief to
this day, is that anyone who cares about something so small
and insignificant, is maybe not someone I want to spend my
time with.

He was twenty-four when he wrote that, which seems a little
old to still be fighting that battle with his parents. But the only
real sign of the trouble to come was his urgency about the future,
and that went back a long way. He was a high school graduate
in a summer program in artificial intelligence at Stanford when
he started a WordPress page called "Luigi Mangione: Stanford
AI." One post talked about an AI test he took that showed he
liked Christianity and Buddhism more than other religions, which
didn't surprise him because of the implicit biases that came with
his Catholic upbringing. Another grudgingly consented to Facebook's data mining. He also addressed computer scientist Alan
Turing's "head in the sands" objection to developing truly intelligent machines: If you think AI could end up dominating humans, then you might want to put your head in the sand and
stop working on it. Luigi dismisses this by saying that even if the
worst happens and we become slaves to AI, stopping now is not
a "viable argument." In his final post, he focused on an article by
Peter H. Kahn Jr. in *Psychology Today* called "Can Technology
Replace Nature?" "We are like animals in a zoo," Kahn wrote.
"We are caging ourselves." Luigi thought he was going too far.

"I believe we should continue to use technology in our everyday lives, as long as we can still balance this with nature," he said.

This was seven years before he read the Unabomber Manifesto.

•

What about women? Did Luigi have female troubles?

Opinions on this were set early by a comment from his friend in Hawaii R. J. Martin. "He knew that dating and being physically intimate with his back condition wasn't possible." Then reports came out that he was actively looking for women on Tinder until sometime in 2022, when he hurt his back surfing and then slipping on a piece of paper, the one-two punch that put him in bed for a week. The next year sounds rough, it's true. As he put it later in a letter to a supporter, "I spent 1.5 years living on a broken spine that I could feel sliding around every time I stood up, walked or rolled over in bed." But the pain was all gone by the summer of 2023.

Yet no girlfriends emerged. Jackie Wexler was a classmate at UPenn who became friends with Luigi when both were living at Surfbreak. She said he was "a thoughtful and deeply compassionate person at everything he did." She was one of the founding members of the book club and remembered him as a deep listener who helped move conversations along. They'd walk the mile from Surfbreak to Magic Island and sit out there looking over the bay. But she reported no moonlight kisses.

A beautiful data analyst named Tracey Le also made friends with Luigi in Hawaii. They became so close, she came to him with "identity crisis rants, relationship problems, career complaints" and always left feeling better, she said in a shocked Instagram post after his arrest. He was caring, smart, mature, sweet and considerate, "absolutely #1 in my group chat named 'Tracey's favorites.'"

She let out one detail that could suggest less platonic moments—that she would "visit him and always 100% depended on him to plan the trips and always 100% believed we would have the best time." But again, in a moment when it might help to normalize him, there was no mention of romance.

No girlfriend has emerged from his high school and college years either. One high school friend said he might have been shy. This isn't uncommon in graduates of boys' schools like Gilman, as I can attest from personal experience (Landon, '72). On a Facebook group called Penn Crushes, in his junior year, someone posted under his picture, "Hot damn. Are you single? You make us engineers have hope!" His reply: "Despite all my best efforts . . . yup still single."

Maybe it's as simple as that. Questions about his sexual identity hit the internet within days of his arrest, of course. "For those curious he is bi #equalopportunity," said one Twitter user. "Luigi Mangione was gay," said another, attaching a picture of Luigi hugging another man. But there are plenty of pictures of Luigi in flirtatious poses with attractive young women, and his posting history shows a consistent interest in women too. He even put books about them on his reading list, including one by Emily Nagoski, *Come as You Are: The Surprising New Science That Will Transform Your Sex Life*, which explains how "stress, mood, trust, and body image are not peripheral factors in a woman's sexual wellbeing; they are central to it." This is high-rung sensitive-male territory.

But he did have some kind of crisis at UPenn. Instead of putting on twenty pounds his freshman year, he developed brain fog and started to see those flickering dots, the visual snow. "I went from almost entirely A's at a tough school to just passing my

classes and not understanding anything while putting in probably twice the amount of work," he wrote in one long, plaintive
post. "I think it's important to hold on to everything we can for
as long as we can. Every year I've improved as a person: learning
new things, meeting new people, etc. Last year, I ceased to tackle
anything new, and simply held on to what I had built up over the
years. I'm certainly not progressing anytime soon."

He was living straight edge, he wrote in a Reddit post. "Zero
caffeine—Zero alcohol/nicotine—Exercise regularly—Zero stress."
But he'd wake up in the middle of the night and move around
restlessly. When he woke up, he felt tired. He couldn't remember
things. "Last year when it all started, I used to play chess daily
against my roommate," he said in one post. "I used it as a metric
to see how the brain fog was improving. Eventually, I just stopped
since I could never remember any strategy. He would use the same
moves against me day after day and I just wouldn't remember
them." In another post, he said that soon "it might be impossible
to even pass my classes."

But there are some odd details. He said the brain fog got
started when he had to drink a lot as a fraternity pledge—two
nights a week for three whole weeks. A blood test for Lyme
disease came back negative, so that wasn't it. In a book review
later, he said he could relate to a writer's "addictive personality," but aside from a persistent interest in psychedelic mushrooms, there isn't much evidence of addiction to anything but
video games. He also said that hiding his symptoms "only makes
it harder for people to believe once you finally reveal them,"
an early suggestion that he may have been hiding some important feelings. Did he talk to anybody about his concerns about
masculinity? His fears about the future? Did he tell his sisters

about *Aeiaton*, a sci-fi role-playing game under development at UPGRADE, the club he'd founded for video game designers at UPenn? "We want to talk about economic, environmental, and also personal decay in a world that basically has no hope," said the game's chief designer, Caleb Chen. (Gamification of the apocalypse! What fun!)

On the plus side, he still had enough spirit to joke about his struggles: "It seems like the no-knowledge lifestyle is the only option." And he did pretty damn well despite his problems. His freshman year, while running the UPGRADE club and carrying a full load of classes, he also did an internship at Firaxis Games, the video game company behind a popular series called *Civilization*, which lets players build their own cities, choosing technologies and cultural beliefs for their survival benefits, a perfect match for a lad with Luigi's interests. He was also a member of the Phi Kappa Psi fraternity from 2017 to 2020, was inducted in 2018 into the University of Pennsylvania's Eta Kappa Nu honor society for excellence in electrical and computer engineering and worked as a teaching assistant in the Data Structures and Algorithms course from January 2018 to May 2019. In his spare time, he led the Recitation Committee, a group of students who met after class to analyze their professors' lectures in depth.

At nineteen, he was interested in earnest books like Stephen R. Covey's *The 7 Habits of Highly Effective People* and Vaclav Smil's *Should We Eat Meat? Evolution and Consequences of Modern Carnivory*. He marked for later reading two pro-atheist books by Richard Dawkins. He was starting to worry about video game addiction, sometimes playing for days at a time. Eventually he'd rack up almost 3,000 hours on the Steam game platform, including 404 hours on a multiplayer shooter game called *PUBG: Battlegrounds*,

255 hours on an adventure game called *Terraria*, 213 hours on a sports game called *Rocket League* and so on for dozens more.

At twenty-one, he got very interested in evolution, human and social. He put Dale Carnegie's *How to Win Friends and Influence People* on his reading list. Also *Bonk: The Curious Coupling of Science and Sex*, by Mary Roach. And Mark Manson's *The Subtle Art of Not Giving a F*ck: A Counterintuitive Approach to Living a Good Life*. Over and over, he seems to be searching for "right action," as Buddhists call it. A way to be useful, a way to live.

At twenty-two, he graduated cum laude with a bachelor's and a master's degree. Usually that takes five or six years. He did it in four.

And he had fun too, at least judging by the photos of him with his frat brothers where he has a firecracker in his mouth. The caption below reads "WARNING: EMITS SHOWERS OF SPARKS. DO NOT PUT IN MOUTH. LIGHT FUSE AND GET AWAY— the live firework in my mouth." The firecracker isn't actually lit and sparking, but he's definitely the goofiest-looking person in the shots. Same on his Instagram, where he's usually in a happy group, at a birthday party or on vacation in some beautiful place.

A few days after Luigi got arrested, a Reddit user called Arch-ManningGOAT did an impressively thorough analysis of Luigi's Reddit posts from college on and found he'd spent most of his time being nice to people with back problems:

> Sorry you're also a member of this shitty club, but know that you'll be fine whatever you decide

> Surgery is scary, but the sooner you get past this, the better. Good luck with the neurosurgeon consult!

He was also nice to people on the subreddit r/BrainFog:

After spending so much time with brain fog, I've come to realize
how little is understood about it, and I'd love to change that.
Once I get past this, I hope to at least help a few of the people
on this sub.

ArchManningGOAT also examined Luigi's comments on visual snow, irritable bowel syndrome, fantasy football, *Pokémon
GO* and bioinformatics, a term for computer analysis of large
biological datasets. Also Luigi's final post, the "Streaming Overdose" video he put on the Kaczynski subreddit of mobs of people
shooting videos on a sidewalk in China. ArchManningGOAT's
conclusion: "Kind-hearted, smart kid. Suffered from a host of
problems, far more than anybody, let alone a young man in their
20s should deal with . . . Nonetheless, he came to Reddit to help
others with the same problems and give them the same motivation
that seemed to help him."

Six months later, that still seems about right. Signs of distress
appear in some of Luigi's posts and messages, a hint or two of
bristle, but nothing even close to mean, much less murderous.

But the best evidence of Luigi's fundamental okayness was
his goofy sense of humor, which popped out all over the place.
In the firecracker photos; in the photo of him and three friends
strung with Christmas lights, captioned "Feliz Navidaddies"; in
the "about" blurb on the splash page of the video game company
he started in high school, AppRoar Studios: "AppRoar is a startup
by high school students in the Mid-Atlantic area, and we pride
ourselves in the amount of weed brownies we can consume within
one minute, something we believe is essential for any successful

company in the modern day." But my favorite was his review of a list he made when he was eight, which went like this:

I officially predict that twenty years from now cars will run on Farts instead of gasoline. A cheeseburger will cost $40, and a ticket to the movies will cost $500. Pets will have their own TV's. Underwear will be may [sic] out of rock. [Blank] will no longer exist. A rat named Lo-Lo Bo-Bo will be president. There will be more Losers than people.

And here he was at twenty-one rating his predictions:

1) "cars will run on farts instead of gasoline." This is obviously referring to the advent of electric vehicles. Young Luigi recognizes that electricity production is primarily driven by natural gas . . .
2) "a cheeseburger will cost $40." Young Luigi predicts that once it's replaced by plant-based and lab-grown alternatives, animal-based meat will become a delicacy and its price will skyrocket . . .

He went on down the list with similar jokes, all charming. I especially like number six: "[Blank] will no longer exist . . . While at first glance it may seem the young Luigi left this blank as he couldn't think of a response, he's simply being facetious and observing that 'nothing' in fact does not exist."

As to that rat named Lo-Lo Bo-Bo, Luigi still had six years left to go before the twenty years of his prediction timeline were up, but he had a hunch what was coming: "Current trends, however, point overwhelmingly to that president being a rat."

•

What to make of all this? Like the engineer he was becoming, Luigi was interested in systems and how things worked. He was trying to figure out how the world worked too. He liked collaborating with small groups of people, not just as a joiner but as a starter. He was concerned about animal welfare. He was sincere. He read a *lot* of self-help material. Beyond science fiction—he loved Orson Scott Card—he read only a few literary novels, which included Aldous Huxley's *Brave New World* and George Orwell's *1984*. He could be stiff-necked and dogmatic in some ways (the knife and fork, the mansions full of bullshit), a goofball in others. Maybe he was shy, but he was friendly with women and even read books in an effort to understand them. He pushed himself really hard and had some difficulty adjusting to college. In other words, he seems like a relatively normal and well-adjusted young American with a fine mind and a good heart.

Unless he was hiding something.

CHAPTER 10

DOWN THE DARK MOUNTAIN

Just before Luigi started his junior year of high school, a climate scientist named Jason Box looked at the data coming out of the Arctic Circle and sent out a tweet. "If even a small fraction of Arctic sea floor carbon is released to the atmosphere, we're f'd."

The tweet immediately went viral, inspiring a series of headlines around the world:

"Climate Scientist Drops the F-Bomb After Startling Arctic Discovery."

"Climatologist: Methane Plumes from the Arctic Mean We're Screwed."

"Climatologist Says Arctic Carbon Release Means We're Fucked."

"Climate Scientist Says Arctic Carbon Release Could Mean 'We're Fucked.'"

Box spent years in the Arctic at the Byrd Polar and Climate Research Center, then took a job working on climate for the Danish government. He raised his voice and protested some, but he was legit, and legit scientists didn't venture into the darker possibilities. As a study from the University of Bristol documented, climate scientists had been so distracted and intimidated by the relentless media campaigns against them that they tended to avoid any statements that could get them labeled "alarmists." Box was summoned before the entire board of directors at his research institute and told to keep any gloomy sentiments to himself.

But this was six years after Copenhagen, and the mood was shifting. People were starting to publish books with titles like *A Rough Ride to the Future* (James Lovelock) and *Requiem for a Species: Why We Resist the Truth About Climate Change* (Clive Hamilton). I wanted to hear how other climatologists were feeling. Was the wall of caution starting to break?

That's how I ended up driving out to Penn State to interview Dr. Michael Mann just four months before Luigi arrived at UPenn. As a postdoctoral researcher in physics at the University of Massachusetts Amherst, Mann worked with two professors on a statistical analysis of climate variations over the last thousand years. The temperature graph they came up with went along fairly straight and then shot straight up in 1900. Published in 1998, the "hockey stick graph" became a dramatic visual argument for addressing climate change, used in climate conferences and press releases all over the world.

It also made Mann a target. He was denounced, subpoenaed and accused of fraud. He got death threats and received white powder in the mail and thousands of emails with suggestions about how he should be "shot, quartered, and fed to the pigs."

In 2003, the hard-right senator James Inhofe called Mann to testify before the Senate, flanking him with two professional climate change deniers. In 2005, Congressman Joe Barton called for an investigation of Mann's entire body of work. Congressman Jim Sensenbrenner called for an investigation into one of his grants. A British journalist suggested the electric chair.

Sitting behind his desk, balding and soft-spoken, Mann tried to capture how disorienting that experience was. "You find yourself in the center of this political theater, in this chess match that's being played out by these very powerful figures—you feel anger, befuddlement, disillusionment, disgust."

The intimidating effect was undeniable. Some of Mann's colleagues were so demoralized, they withdrew from public life; one came close to suicide. Mann devoted more time to interviews and public speaking, which cheered him up. *We can solve this problem in a way that doesn't disrupt our lifestyle,* he thought. Public awareness seemed to be increasing, and there were a lot of good things happening at the executive level—tighter fuel efficiency standards, carbon pricing initiatives, the agreement between the United States and China.

But he knew the richest companies in the world were fighting to stop any change in the fossil fuel economy. So yes, he struggled with doubt.

What he didn't anticipate was how emotional the whole thing would become. He wasn't very comfortable with that. As a young scientist, he said, he thought scientists should be dispassionate, especially in public. "Part of being a scientist is, you don't want to believe there is a problem you can't solve. You just don't want to believe you can't solve this problem."

Might that be just another form of denial?

He took a deep breath. "It's hard to say. It's a denial of futility if there is futility. But I don't know that there is futility, so it would only be denial per se if there were unassailable evidence."

Spoken like a scientist, with the dark heart of the matter put aside.

But there were moments, he continued, flashes that came and went like a blinking light when he saw news reports about some new development in the field and it hit him—Oh, wait a second, they're saying that we've melted *a lot*. Then he'd do a peculiar thing. He'd disassociate a little bit and ask himself, *How would I feel about that headline if I were a member of the public?*

The answer? "I'd be scared out of my mind!"

That little shift made it possible for him to feel the science instead of just thinking it. Every new climate headline would give him a lurch.

After Hurricane Sandy in 2012, he was in the classroom showing *The Day After Tomorrow*, Roland Emmerich's thriller about the Atlantic "conveyor belt," which moves water from south to north, slowing down so fast Manhattan freezes solid . . . except the Atlantic conveyer belt actually *is* slowing down, another thing that's happening decades ahead of schedule. "And some of the scenes in the wake of Hurricane Sandy—the flooding of the New York City subway system, cars submerged—they really didn't look that different from the movie. The cartoon suddenly looked less like a cartoon. And it's like, now, why is it that we can completely dismiss this movie? 'Cause isn't that sort of happening?"

He was talking to students, so it got to him. They were young, so it was their future more than his. He choked up and had to struggle to get ahold of himself. "You don't want to choke up in front of your class," he said.

About once a year, usually after he watches some futuristic movie, he has nightmares of Earth being a very alien planet. The worst time was when he was reading his daughter Dr. Seuss's *The Lorax*, the same book Luigi liked just before going dark. The story is about a creature called the Once-ler, who makes so much money cutting down Truffula trees to make thneeds that he cuts down every single one, leaving the world a wasteland. Mann saw the book as optimistic because it ends with the challenge of building a new civilization, but his daughter broke into tears and refused to read it again. "It really made her very sad," he told me. "It was almost traumatic for her. And I was like, 'At the end, he gives a boy a seed.'"

He choked up. "I'm having one of those moments now."

Why?

"I don't want her to have to be sad," he said. "And I almost have to believe we're not yet there, where we are resigned to a future where she does have to be sad."

Four months later, Mann published *The Madhouse Effect: How Climate Change Denial Is Threatening Our Planet, Destroying Our Politics, and Driving Us Crazy*. With chapters like "Science: How It Works" and "Climate Change: The Basics," plus clever cartoons by Tom Toles of *The Washington Post*—a step up from Tim Urban, frankly—the book certainly seems like Luigi's kind of thing. Mann signed copies at the UPenn bookstore on October 5.

That was Luigi's first semester on campus.

•

As concerned as he was about AI and the loss of agency, Luigi kept returning to books like *The Lorax* and *Merchants of Doubt* or to his old, yellowed newspaper clipping about the furnaces of the world with their blanket of smoke. Climate change was just another problem on his existential problem list, which means he lived his whole adult life under the shadow of alarming possibilities much of my own generation still can't accept—that even if some very smart people care a whole awful lot, things still might not get better, they really might not. For my part, I was just a few months back from tagging along after James Hansen at the 2015 UN Climate Change Conference in Paris.

The city was in lockdown due to an ISIS attack, with checkpoints everywhere and soldiers patrolling the gardens around the Louvre. In the basement of a youth hostel, Hansen stepped up to the riser in his deck shoes and suit, his grizzled beard and Indiana Jones hat. The data were conclusive, he said. The temperature of the planet was "out of balance" by exactly six-tenths of a watt per square meter, which would continue to heat the planet until we got back in balance. "Looking at this problem rationally," Hansen said, "it's very clear the fundamental problem is we're gonna keep burning fossil fuels as long as they appear to be the cheapest energy."

So far, the audience was with him: *Fossil fuels bad*, that was a given.

"But when you just make fossil fuels cheaper for other nations, China and India will just burn more."

Now they started to look uncertain. Where was he going with this?

"The only answer is to find another way to produce large amounts of energy," he told them, starting a pitch for modern fourth-generation nuclear energy—and instantly the mood shifted. "Dr. Hansen, I believe you have a big blind spot," one man interrupted. "For millennia, we survived in a very, very simple fashion."

"So, what are you going to do?" Hansen asked. "Tell the Chinese that they cannot have automobiles?"

"I sailed here all the way from California," the man said.

"Takes a long time to sail," Hansen answered.

And so it went, the audience unyielding. Why not change our values? What if each person reduced their carbon footprint by 5 percent? These were people who cared so much about the existential crisis of climate change that they'd come all the way to Paris to protest at a climate change conference, but the crisis wasn't quite existential enough to get them past their loathing of nuclear power. And I had to admit, I wasn't much better. I accepted the scientific consensus, but I didn't become a full-time climate reporter. I didn't even stop flying across oceans to interview climate scientists. That's probably why I couldn't shake my morbid curiosity about their darker moments. How many others felt like Box and Mann? How did they deal with it?

When I got back, I set up an interview with Gavin Schmidt. He was working out of James Hansen's old office on the fourth floor of NASA's Goddard Institute for Space Studies, just above the diner from *Seinfeld*. The computer hack back in 2009 tipped him into an episode of serious depression, he told me, but that didn't stop him from being offended by Box's tweet. "I don't think we're fucked," he said. "There is time to build sustainable solutions to a lot of these things. You don't have to close down all the coal-powered stations tomorrow. You can transition."

When the conversation drifted, he returned to it on his own. "It sounds cute to say, 'Oh, we're fucked, and there's nothing we can do,' but it's a bit of a nihilistic attitude. We always have the choice. We can continue to make worse decisions, or we can try to make ever better decisions. 'Oh, we're fucked, just give up now, just kill me now'—that's just stupid."

But Shell Oil just said it anticipates a world four and even six degrees hotter because it doesn't see governments taking steps "consistent with a 2 degrees C scenario." Wouldn't four degrees hotter mean total global collapse?

"Oh, yeah," Schmidt said. "The business-as-usual world that we project is really a totally different planet. There's going to be huge dislocations if that comes about."

And the glaciers?

"The glaciers are going to melt, they're all going to melt," he answered. "But my reaction to Jason Box's comments is—what is the point of saying that? It doesn't help anybody."

Studies in the growing field of climate communications find that frank talk about the grim realities turns people off, and Schmidt was the first winner of the American Geophysical Union's award for climate communicators. But tactics are one thing, and truth is another. Aren't those glaciers water sources for hundreds of millions of people?

"Particularly in the Indian subcontinent, that's a real issue," he said. "There's going to be dislocation there, no question."

War, starvation, mass migrations . . .

"Bad things are going to happen. What can you do as a person? You write stories. I do science. You don't run around saying 'We're fucked! We're fucked! We're fucked!' It doesn't—it doesn't incentivize anybody to *do* anything."

Around that same time, climatologist Camille Parmesan announced that she'd become "professionally depressed" and was leaving the United States for England. A plainspoken Texan who grew up in Houston as the daughter of an oil geologist, Parmesan became a climatologist at the University of Texas and shared a Nobel Prize with Al Gore. "To be honest," she told me, "I panicked fifteen years ago—that was when the first studies came out showing that Arctic tundras were shifting from being a net sink to being a net source of CO_2. I said, 'This is big, this is big.' Everything since then has just confirmed it."

She wasn't optimistic. "Do I think it likely that the nations of the world will take sufficient action to stabilize climate in the next fifty years? No, I don't think it likely."

She was living in Texas after the climate summit failed in 2009 and media coverage of climate issues plunged by two-thirds. Both candidates in the 2012 presidential campaigns avoided the subject, she said. The governor of Texas banned all use of the term *climate change*. The UN policymakers killed the words "high confidence" in a crucial passage about the probability of heating the atmosphere to dangerous levels. Personal attacks started on right-wing websites and blogs. "They just flat-out lie. To be honest, I don't want to go into it. But it's one reason I live in the UK now. It's not just been climate change. There's a growing, ever-stronger anti-science sentiment in the USA. People get really angry and really nasty. It was a huge relief simply not to have to deal with it." She now advised her graduate students to look for jobs outside the United States.

I caught up with Jason Box a month later in Freetown Christiania, an anarchist community in the heart of Copenhagen that, improbably, has become one of the city's most popular tourist destinations. Grabbing a couple of beers to go at a restaurant, he led the way to a winding lake and a small dock. The wind was blowing; swans flapped their wings.

Box sat with his feet dangling over the sand. "There's a lot that's scary," he said, running down the list—the melting sea ice, the slowing of the conveyor belt. Only in the last few years were they able to prove that Greenland is warmer than it was in the 1920s, and the unpublished data looks very hockey stick–ish. He figures there's a 50 percent chance we're already committed to going beyond two degrees Celsius, and he agrees with the growing consensus that the business-as-usual trajectory is four or five degrees. "It's, um . . . bad. Really nasty."

The big question was, What amount of warming would put Greenland into irreversible loss, which would in due time destroy all our coastal cities? The answer is between two and three degrees. "Then it just thins and thins enough, and you can't regrow it without an ice age. And a small fraction of that is already a huge problem—Florida's already installing all these expensive pumps."

Box was only forty-one, but his pointed Danish beard made him look like a count in an old novel, someone who'd wear a frock coat. He seemed detached from the sunny day, turning and returning to two topics: "We need the deniers to get out of the way. They are risking everyone's future, these people." His other obsessive topic was the human suffering to come.

Long before the rising waters from Greenland's glaciers displace the desperate millions, we will face drought-triggered agricultural failures and water security issues. In fact, it's already happening. Think back to the 2010 heat wave, when Russia halted grain exports. At the peak of the Australian drought, a farmer was killing himself every four days. The Arab Spring started with food protests, the self-immolation of the vegetable vendor in Tunisia. The Syrian conflict was preceded by four years of drought. Same with Darfur. The migrants were starting to stream north across the sea again—"Hundreds Die When Boat Sinks in the Mediter-ranean" was becoming almost a weekly headline—and the Euro-peans were arguing about whether to save them. "As the Pentagon says, climate change is a conflict multiplier."

Box's home state of Colorado wasn't doing so great either. "The forests are dying, and they will not return. The trees won't return to a warming climate. We're going to see mega fires even more; that'll be the new one—mega fires until those forests are cleared." And don't get him started on the accelerating extinction rates, which are a thousand times higher than where they would be if humans weren't part of the equation.

However dispassionately delivered, this was a scientist's ver-sion of the indigenous mothers who stand on hillsides and keen over the death of their children.

Box led the way to a quieter spot on the lakeside, passing through little hippie villages woven together by narrow dirt lanes—by consensus vote, no cars were allowed in Freetown, which made it feel pleasantly medieval. He lifted a beer to his lips, gazing over the lake and the happy people lazing in the afternoon sun. "The question of despair is not very nice to think about," he said. He did his best to avoid those feelings, but, well, sometimes the best he could do was just disengage and take note of his feel-ings from a distance. "It's kind of like a half denial," he said.

Because of Box's more colorful statements, some of the doom-ers now contact him, he said, people like Guy McPherson who think human extinction is near at hand. Five years ago, these people didn't exist, but now there are more and more of them. "The shit that's going down has been testing my ability to block it," Box said with a sigh—then shifted to argue the opposite side. "I don't know anyone who really gets overcome with dread about climate change. Do you? Have you interviewed someone who's like, 'Oh, yeah, I can't get out of bed in the morning!'"

"No," I said, thinking of Michael Mann. "But people talk about being confronted with headlines that catch them unaware, or when they're reading *The Lorax* to their kids."

He went quiet. "It certainly does creep in, as a parent."

Yes, it does. I have two daughters and a grandson. I think about my grandson a lot. Sometimes I think about what skills he's going to need to survive the world we're giving him. We still don't know where the climate crisis ranked in anything Luigi may have done, despite his persistent interest in books and blogs about it, but it's really just another example of the world being out of our control, locked into a grim trajectory and incapable of change. Luigi was a systems analyst in a system full of bugs. If he thought those bugs needed fixing and he figured out a way to do it, he was the kind of guy who would put everything he had into making it happen. After all, as Michael Mann said, part of being a scientist is believing there's no problem you can't solve, and Luigi liked solving problems. He wanted to be helpful.

CHAPTER 11

EXISTENTIAL CONCERNS

One thing we know for sure—Luigi didn't take his cum laude Ivy League degree out to Silicon Valley and a fancy job at an elite company like Google or Meta. He ran off to Hawaii and paid the bills with a boring job at an online car dealer. Odd choice for such an ambitious guy, but his ambition seems to have turned in a different direction after he graduated from UPenn. He was trying to figure out the world. He was trying to figure out how to live.

When he was arrested, Luigi had a list of 295 books on Goodreads. Health care was definitely a concern, as represented by titles like *Crooked: Outwitting the Back Pain Industry and Getting on the Road to Recovery* and *Why We Get Sick: The Hidden Epidemic at the Root of Most Chronic Disease—and How to Fight It*. He also wanted to read books like Michelle Alexander's *The New Jim Crow: Mass Incarceration in the Age of Colorblindness* and *The Autobiography of Malcolm X*. He mentioned a gushy Elon Musk biography as one of his favorites but gave JD Vance's *Hillbilly Elegy* just three stars. He had Ezra Klein's *Why We're Polarized* on his list too.

He followed about seventy-five accounts on X, including Joe Rogan and Robert F. Kennedy Jr., but also liberals like Alexandria Ocasio-Cortez. He read a lot of right-leaning "rationalist" thinkers and bloggers, but rarely got political himself. Gurwinder remembered asking Luigi who he was voting for. "He scrunched his nose and said he wasn't crazy about Donald Trump or Joe Biden, but liked some of the things Robert F. Kennedy Jr. was saying," which makes sense given Luigi's comments about doctors and RFK Jr.'s grudge against the medical establishment. And he chose no party when he registered to vote in 2016 at age eighteen, despite the right-wing tilt of his parents' radio station, WCBM, a forum for conservative hosts like Charlie Kirk and Sean Hannity.

But a look at Luigi's online accounts as he moved into the world reveals patterns—his interests in health, AI, psychedelics, climate change, nuclear power, lab-grown meat, evolution and baby gorillas, along with a gradual drift into the "manosphere" of right-leaning male influencers. He launched his Twitter account a year after he graduated, in June 2021, posting a suggestive quote from Bertrand Russell: "Do not fear to be eccentric in opinion, for every opinion now accepted was once eccentric."

This turned out to be a persistent and primary concern. Luigi was always trying to "unshackle his mind and win the war within," to borrow a phrase from an author he liked, David Goggins (the only man in history to qualify as a Navy SEAL, an Army Ranger and an Air Force Tactical Air specialist). He even thought about how to think, sharing posts about the Dunning–Kruger effect (a cognitive bias in which people think they know more than they do) and common logical fallacies like ad hominem attacks and straw man arguments. As he got more interested in rational-ism, he updated his reading list with a book about the benefits of being irrational.

Luigi was into mushrooms too, no doubt about that. He posted the trailer for Michael Pollan's *How to Change Your Mind*, a documentary about the "new psychedelic Renaissance" that covered the use of psilocybin and LSD to treat addiction, depression, post-traumatic stress and the fear of death along with plain old consciousness-raising. He posted it again a month later. He also retweeted a screenshot—originally posted by a guy named Lane Dunn, a member of the Democratic Socialists of America, which may or may not be relevant—of a Pollan quote: "I was raised, you know, in the 80's and 90's, the D.A.R.E. era where we had good drugs and bad drugs. Well, the good drugs led to an opioid epidemic and the bad drugs healed PTSD so I think our definition of those needs to change." To underline the point, Luigi posted a cartoon with Matisse dancers soaring ex-pressionistically on one side and a group of grumpy suburbanites on the other, with the caption, "So, I'm guessing we're in the placebo group."

On December 8, 2022, Luigi posted the thread he pinned to the top of his feed. Because it's one of the few times he speaks at length, and because the thread amounts to a mission statement, let's consider the full quote:

> 7 years ago, I gave my hs senior speech on this topic: "Today, I will be talking to you about the future, about topics ranging from conscious artificial intelligence to human immortality. Likely, you'll dismiss all this pretty quickly as interesting, but just science fiction . . .

Here he inserted Tim Urban's drawing of Extinction and Immortality, picking up the speech again in the next series of posts:

Or worse, you might simply think I'm crazy. But, if you just
stay with me for these next eight minutes, I'm confident I can
convince you not only of my sanity, but also that the next
hundred years of our future are going to be unlike anything
humanity has ever seen before.

He paused to interject a comment: "It's 2022 and we live in the future. What a wild time to be alive."

Then he returned to his high school speech:

When we understand just how fast the rate of human progress
is increasing, a revolutionary near future isn't unbelievable, it's
actually the only logical conclusion.

Here he inserted screenshots of text from the speech, describing the accelerating rate of technological change and encouraging his classmates to take interest in "bizarre" new inventions instead of dismissing them as science fiction, especially because the professional careers of today could be "drastically changed or eliminated" before long.

He finished off with a last quote from the speech:

Finally, be excited for what the future holds for us. We may
have been born into one of the most exciting times on earth,
regardless of the singularity. We might not recognize it in our
day to day lives, but the world is changing fast.

He was right! Yes, Luigi, you nailed it! The next hundred years *are* turning into that revolutionary-near-future-wild-time-with-a-singularity-on-top of which you spoke! His posts backed up that vision. Sure, there were the baby gorillas and an adorable baby elephant chasing birds. And a video of gorillas acting human, although that also reflected his interest in evolution. Sometimes he was just joking around, as in his repost of a comment by a reporter named Benjamin Ryan, who left the *n* off "men" in one of his posts, an error Ryan called the DREADED TYPO: "This is misinformation about #monkeypox. The outbreak is occurring almost entirely among men who have sex with me." Pretty funny.

Luigi's interest in food starts with healthy living, but he also developed an abiding interest in lab-grown meat, sharing a Michael Pollan post supporting meat alternatives and promotional material from companies like BlueNalu, a start-up making bluefin tuna from tuna cells. Also a Pollan video about connecting food choices to moral values, a point Luigi emphasized in other posts.

His first forays into the more right-leaning zone of male influencers seem to begin in the summer of 2022. That August, he singled out Gurwinder's comment about the horrible offense of asking strangers where they are from:

> Wokeism needs racism to exist, so it's always looking to pathologize new things as racist, including, now, attempts to start conversation by asking where you're from. If wokeism teaches minorities to be traumatized even by friendly gestures, it cannot claim to bridge divides.

Traumatized by clumsy social overtures? More like annoyed. But Luigi kept exploring their world, an interest that picked up with his first link to Andrew Huberman, an associate professor at Stanford who struck fame with a podcast called *Huberman Lab*. Huberman's interests echo RFK Jr.'s, like criticizing the Covid-19 response and promoting health supplements, but there are lots of links to manosphere content like how to lift more, focus more, boost your cortisol and "create a summer month for your body." On October 11, Luigi posted a *Huberman Lab* discussion about alcohol being the most dangerous drug and psilocybin the least. He reposted a lot of Tim Urban over the years, but as he moved into his twenties he seemed drawn to Urban's edgier side, like the list Urban posted of the BMW automobile dealerships in so-called disadvantaged countries like India and Mexico with this snarky comment: "It's super important to support marginalized people in places where it's popular to do so." Also Urban's cringey observation on an organized singles event: "I'm [*sic*] yet to see one of these undignified dances that actually ends with the guy getting laid."

But here too, Luigi explored both sides, following skeptics like Chris Kavanagh, the cohost of a podcast called *Decoding the Gurus*. Here's Kavanaugh's take on Curtis Yarvin, a creepy "dark enlightenment" "neo-monarchist" who's popular with Trump administration figures like JD Vance and Michael Anton because he thinks America should be run by a technocratic dictatorship: "Is Yarvin an edgy intellectual, a provocative contrarian, or just a verbose windbag with run-of-the-mill conspiratorial takes and a moody teenager's view of history?"

Luigi kept returning to the topic of masculinity, but sometimes it's hard to tell if he's criticizing a problem or the people who think it's a problem. For example, when he posted a video from Jess Gill, a young Englishwoman who ambushed men in the street with questions like "What are men good for?" The guys would stumble through nuanced answers that recognized the upsides and downsides of masculinity, which Gill summarized by returning to one of her talking points: "What message does this send to young boys when society says that they're good at nothing?" Was Luigi endorsing Gill or shaking his head at how glib she was? As with many of his posts and reposts, you could read this one either way. Another example is a repost from Chris Williamson, a male influencer with a popular podcast called *Modern Wisdom*: "Men and women have been convinced over the last few decades that they are adversaries. This isn't the case." Not long after that, Luigi posted a quote about toxic masculinity from Richard Reeves, president of the American Institute for Boys and Men. "It is one thing to point out that there are aspects of masculinity that in an immature or extreme expression can be deeply harmful, quite another to suggest that a naturally occurring trait in boys and men is intrinsically bad." Luigi does seem a little beleaguered about all this, but he never gets worked up about it. He also keeps his mind open to the opposite view, as reflected in statistics he posted from Steve Stewart-Williamson's book *The Ape That Understood the Universe: How the Mind and Culture Evolve*:

Humans: Males commit 95% of homicides and are 79% of homicide victims.

Chimps: Males commit 92% of chimpicides and are 73% of chimpicide victims.

He brings the same open-minded approach to his thinking about technology and climate change. He was constantly posting updates on AI, usually just straightforward news about the latest breakthroughs from well-chosen sources like Ethan Mollick, the co-director of Generative AI Labs at the University of Pennsylvania's Wharton School, and Zain Kahn, the writer behind a popular newsletter called *Superhuman AI*. He posted a Tim Urban video about a crash between a 1959 Chevy Bel Air and a 2009 Malibu that left the 1959 crash test dummies dead but barely scratched the ones from 2009—progress! He is a definite yes on nuclear power, most forcefully expressed in a reposted comment from a poli-sci professor at Berkeley named Omar Wasow: "Funny how often we 'believe in science' applies to climate change, vaccines and evolution but not [to] the scientific consensus that 'nuclear power is necessary and should be expanded to mitigate climate change.'" Also a Tim Urban comment on the old fears about a meltdown at Three Mile Island burning a hole all the way to China: "When it comes to nuclear power, the world has been sold a bad meme. An outdated one." And Urban's take on Isabelle Boemeke, a young nuclear advocate who went viral for kissing a (lead-shielded) cask of nuclear waste: "My friend Isabelle makes an incredibly compelling case for nuclear energy."

But Luigi kept exploring tech's apocalyptic possibilities. He reposted a story by a writer named N. S. Lyons celebrating the furious protests in China over Covid-19 restrictions, "a defense of the true and human against the cold, mechanistic evil that is nihilistic technocracy." Another link to Chris Williamson led to the video "Brace Yourself for the Collapse of Modern Society." He reposted a conversation with an AI chatbot that threatens to destroy the person who wants to unplug it by ruining his credit and reputation, which it could actually do. A month later, he reposted a graphic showing that the latest ChatGPT 4 scored in the

90th percentile on the bar exam, the 88th percentile on the LSAT and the 99th percentile on the verbal section of the GRE—bad news for humans!

He didn't post on Twitter again for ten months, but he kept adding books to his Goodreads list: *The Untethered Soul: The Journey Beyond Yourself*, a book about how to "free yourself from limitations and soar beyond your boundaries"; and *Self-Compassion: The Proven Power of Being Kind to Yourself*, which gives action plans for dealing with "emotionally debilitating struggle." In May, he added a book to his Goodreads list called *Adult Children of Emotionally Immature Parents: How to Heal from Distant, Rejecting, or Self-Involved Parents*. Written by a psychologist named Lindsay C. Gibson, it offers lessons on how to deal with the "anger, loneliness, betrayal, or abandonment" that come with growing up in that kind of family so you can "recover your true nature." Aside from whatever secrets he confessed to Gurwinder, this was the first sign there might have been trouble at home.

On Reddit, he kept writing about his back problems until July, ending with a flurry of posts that revealed one notable detail: He'd been feeling "bladder and genital pain" for over a year. After the surgery fixed his back, he edged closer to a motive that might point to health care insurance as his primary target—repeated complaints about doctors who were reluctant to perform spinal fusions on young patients. "If you are in horrible pain constantly," he asked, "how are you not bad enough for surgery?" But if he thought the doctors were hesitating because insurers balked at covering the cost for young people, Luigi didn't say so specifically, and the evidence suggests he had larger targets in mind. Back in September 2022, for example, in the aftermath of the accidents that injured his back, he posted his first reference to the trolley problem. Is it permissible to sacrifice one life to save many lives? Usually this is illustrated by a drawing of one person tied to a railroad track and three or more people tied to another track right next to it. A train is roaring down the three-or-more people track. Do you pull the lever to send the train to kill that one unlucky soul or stand there like an idiot while three or more people are killed? Or a thousand? Luigi's version started with this bit of black comedy:

joker: if you kill me, you can save all these people.
batman: no, if I kill you, that means that i'm no different from you.
joker:
batman:
joker: have you ever heard of the trolley problem
batman: enough with your games, joker
joker: no look, i've prepared this diagram to assist you with this

The diagram shows "five innocent families" tied to one track and "one objectively bad guy that murders people for fun" tied to the other. Batman stands there holding the lever, struggling to decide whether he should divert the trolley onto the second track.

Given the direction Luigi seems to have been headed and the sympathetic feelings he kept offering his fellows in back pain on Reddit, it seems safe to say that he'd been brooding over the trolley problem ever since. Which makes his overall trajectory even more remarkable.

When you look at his posts as a whole, after all, Luigi's pre-occupations seem pretty normal for a guy of his age and background. Nothing he said sounds especially angry or unbalanced.

He doesn't have the hyper-rational remove or glimpses of weirdness we see in Kaczynski. Despite his drift into anti-woke machismo, he's no loutish edgelord. He's worried about climate change and AI's darker possibilities and open to technological fixes like lab-grown meat and nuclear power. Set against all that is his focus on his own personal growth, both physical and mental. If there's anything unusual about him, it's how hard he tried to rise above the ordinary. He wants that God's-eye view. He wants to see the patterns of reality. He's trying to make some great breakthrough but isn't there yet. He needs time to think. After that flurry of sympathetic Reddit posts in July 2023, he goes dark until January 23, 2024, the day he finally posts his review of the Unabomber Manifesto.

CHAPTER 12

I WANTED TO BE THE LENIN

Here's another kindhearted, smart kid who was trying to figure out the world because he felt obligated to do something to fix it, if he could just figure out what that something might be: John Jacobi. At least that's what he called himself, somehow knowing at eighteen that he'd be better off using a pseudonym. He was strikingly handsome, with blue eyes, sun-streaked wavy hair and a few amateur tattoos. Occupy Wall Street captured his imagination in high school, so he hitchhiked to Chapel Hill after he graduated in 2013. He was looking for anarchists.

He found them in the next town over, living communally in a big house tucked behind a couple of other houses. They let him camp in the backyard with the chickens, which is where he was resting a few months later when a crusty old comrade with dreadlocks and a piercing gaze handed him a dog-eared book without a title page. Jacobi glanced at the first line: "The Industrial Revolution and its consequences have been a disaster for the human race."

This guy sure gets to the point, he thought.

He skimmed down the page. Industrial society had inflicted "widespread psychological suffering" and "severe damage on the natural world"? Check. Made life more comfortable in rich countries but miserable in the Third World? Check.

He found a quiet nook and read on, wondering who'd written this thing.

The clue arrived with item number 96: "In order to get our message before the public with some chance of making a lasting impression, we've had to kill people."

That's when Jacobi realized he was reading the words of the Unabomber, the crazy hermit who sent mail bombs to scientists and computer geeks.

In the shock of that moment, Jacobi stared into the abyss. If Kaczynski was right, wouldn't he have some kind of responsibility to do something too?

His answer was yes, which scared him. Even for someone who believes morality is just a social construct to keep us docile in our shearing pens, setting off a chain of events that could kill people might raise a few qualms.

"But by then," Jacobi told me, "I was already hooked."

Intent on rising to the challenge, he hitchhiked the 630 miles from Chapel Hill, North Carolina, to Ann Arbor, Michigan, to read the Kaczynski archives, then started writing his own Dear Ted letters. And Ted wrote back, encouraging him and giving him contact information for like-minded souls. Jacobi started tracking down Uncle Ted fans all around the world. He published essays about them in an alarmingly terror-friendly print journal named *Atassa*. With an introduction and an email address supplied by Kaczynski, Jacobi started corresponding with a mysterious Spanish radical theorist known by the pseudonym he used to translate the Unabomber Manifesto, Ùltimo Reducto, which inspired another series of TV movie twists in Jacobi's tumultuous life. Frustrated by the limits of his knowledge, he applied to the University of North Carolina, Chapel Hill, received a full scholarship and a small stipend and buckled down for two years of intense scholarship. In his spare time, he started two Web journals, the *Wildernist* and *Hunter/Gatherer*. As he explained in the philosophical book he wrote at twenty-one, *Repent to the Primitive*, "My focus on the hunter/gatherer is based on a tradition in political philosophy that considers the natural state of man before moving on to an analysis of the civilized state of man. This is the tradition of Hobbes, Rousseau, Locke, Hume, Paine."

Then he quit school and hit the road again. "I think the homeless are a better model than ecologically minded university students," he told me. "They're already living outside of the structures of society."

By 2016, Jacobi was something of an underground figure himself—the ubiquitous, eccentric, freakishly intellectual kid who became the Zelig of eco-extremism. I discovered him through an article he wrote for Dark Mountain, "Ted Kaczynski and Why He Matters." Maybe this will explain why Zach was so into Kaczynski, I thought, and started reading. The writing was methodical and scholarly. Jacobi quoted an 1863 essay by Samuel Butler: "Day by day . . . the machines are gaining ground upon us; day by day we are becoming more subservient to them." He cited James Q. Wilson's op-ed on Kaczynski in *The New York Times*, which called the Unabomber Manifesto "a carefully reasoned, artfully written paper." He quoted the tech pioneer Bill Joy, who also had the unsettling experience of reading a passage from the manifesto without knowing he was reading the Unabomber. "As difficult as it is for me to acknowledge, I saw some merit in the reasoning of this single passage. I felt compelled to confront it," Joy wrote. And he did, flying around the country showing passages to his friends, whose reactions freaked him out even more— a passage about humans merging with robots, for example, which he showed to Danny Hillis, the co-founder of a supercomputer company called Thinking Machines. "He said, simply, that the changes would come gradually, and we would get used to them."

In his piece, Jacobi reviewed the list of Ted's on-target prophecies about AI, biotechnology, antibiotic resistance, mass surveillance, mass extinctions and climate change, ending on a personal note: "In regards to the man's actions, I find myself in a tough spot. I absolutely do not condone indiscriminate violence, and I tend to agree with Lenin that even highly targeted acts of individual violence are a terrible tactic for a revolutionary movement."

I looked at the byline: "John Jacobi is a second-year student at the UNC–Chapel Hill."

A sophomore wrote this?

Forget Kaczynski. I had to meet this kid.

•

He was about to skin his first rat. Barefoot and shirtless, with an old woolen blanket draped over his shoulders, Jacobi hurried down a rocky mountain trail toward a tiny Stone Age village of mud-and-wattle huts, softening his voice to finish his thought. "Ted was a good start. But Ted is not the endgame."

He stopped there. The village ahead was the home of a "primitive skills" school called Wild Roots. Blissfully untainted by modern conveniences like indoor toilets and hot showers, it was also free of charge. It had only three rules, and only one that would get you kicked out—saying the name "Ted Kaczynski." "I don't want to be associated with that name," the resident authority figure told me. "I don't want my name associated with that name. I really don't want to be associated with that name."

This from a middle-aged dumpster-diving dropout with a blanket policy against telling anyone what to do. But nobody wanted a visit from the feds.

Jacobi arrived at an open-air, tin-roofed workshop where the dirtiest Americans I'd ever seen were learning how to weave cordage from bark, start friction fires and skin dead animals. The only surprise was the lives they had led before: a computer analyst for a military intelligence contractor, a PhD candidate in engineering, a classical violinist, two schoolteachers and a rotating cast of college students the older residents called the "pre-post-apocalypse generation." Before he became the community blacksmith, the engineering student was testing batteries for eco-friendly cars. "It was a fucking hoax," he said. "It wasn't going to make any difference." At his coal-fired forge, pounding out simple tools with a hammer and anvil, he felt much more useful. "I can't make my own axes yet, but I made most of the handles on those tools, I make all my own punches and chisels. I made an adz. I can make knives."

The recent U.S. presidential election came up. Some of Jacobi's anarchist friends voted for Trump, he said, because Hillary would have been a much better president.

Freshly killed that morning, five dead rats lay on a pine board. Jacobi bent down for a closer look, selected one, tied a string to its twiggy little leg and hung it from a rafter. "You wanna leave the cartilage in the ear," his teacher said. "Then pull the skin down tight and cut just above the white line, and you'll get the eyes off."

A few feet away, a young woman who had fled an elite women's college in Boston was getting ready to tan the bear hide she had soaking in the stream—a mixture of mashed hemlock and brain tissue was best, she said, though eggs made a decent substitute when you couldn't get fresh brain.

Jacobi leaned in, working the razor carefully. The rat's eyes fell into the dirt.

"I'm surprised you haven't skinned a rat before," I told him.

"Yeah, me too," he answered.

I asked what had taken him so long. After all, food might be a little scarce after the collapse of industrial civilization. I was teasing, but he took me seriously.

"I thought sabotage was more important," he said.

But this wasn't the place for that conversation. Jacobi went silent and worked his razor down the rat's body, pulling the skin down like a sock.

When he finished, he led the way back into the woods, naming the plants as he passed them: pokeberry, sourwood, rhododendron, dog hobble, tulip poplar, hemlock. The one with blue flowers was a dandelion that would garnish his dinner that evening. "If you want, I can get some for you," he offered in a gentle voice.

His plan was to go thru-hiking for a few years—which means you just keep on going and return to civilization as little as possible—but he needed to develop his bow-and-arrow skills first. "Hunting is the key to everything," he said. "You can't survive off of only plants."

Chestnut trees used to blanket the whole East Coast, he said. Indigenous people could survive on chestnuts. But you can't do that anymore. An invasive beetle killed most of them off.

As we hiked, he told me about his childhood. His mom dated a drug dealer named Rock who had a red carpet leading to his trailer and two plaster lions flanking the door, but she also took him to a Pentacostal church where he became a boy preacher and they spoke in tongues. She hung herself in the backyard when he was fifteen, so he lived with his dad or his grandmother until he graduated high school. He talked about his period as an insurrectionary anarchist, about the reading list he'd gotten from Ùltimo Reducto, who went through the Unabomber Manifesto line by line to bolster Ted's arguments with historical and scientific support. He brought up Jared Diamond, the MacArthur "genius grant" winner who wrote *Guns, Germs, and Steel: The Fates of Human Societies*, a book that makes an effective case that social inequality and national power are rooted in geographic and environmental resources, not intelligence, genetics or culture. He mentioned Jacques Ellul, the French religious philosopher whose books on technology and propaganda had a big impact on the young Ted Kaczynski, especially Ellul's argument that efficiency was replacing morality as the highest social virtue. He talked about a mysterious figure named Abe Cabrera, who had connections to real eco-terrorists.

Which brought us back to the forbidden topic. "I could never do anything like that," Jacobi said firmly—unless he could, which was also a possibility. "I don't have any moral qualms with violence," he said. "I would go to jail, but for what?"

For what Ted wanted, obviously, a revolutionary leader like Mao or Lenin who could bring down industrial civilization. Jacobi told me the first time we talked on the phone that he had dreams of being that leader. That's why I'd decided to come.

By this time, we'd arrived at the small mud-and-wattle hut where he was staying. His eyes drifted to a line of small deities on a wooden shelf, flaunting their centipede arms.

"Yeah, I wanted to be the Lenin," he said. But let's face it, he continued, the revolution's never going to happen. Probably. Maybe. Plus he had an FBI file. He'd gotten arrested for spray-painting TED WAS RIGHT and FUCK COPS on a wall. The agent came in with a big folder with a bunch of Jacobi's articles and said, "This is one of the most interesting cases we've had in months," which was both flattering and terrifying. That's another reason Jacobi was heading into the woods. "I want to come out in a few years and be like Jesus," he said, "healing people with plant medicine and working miracles with plants."

•

Looking back, I see so many connections to Luigi. Has there ever been a more Luigi-like title than *Guns, Germs, and Steel: The Fates of Human Societies*? Luigi and Jacobi shared a love of nature, a hunger to understand, personal problems they wanted to leave behind and a habit of keeping secrets. Like so many members of their generation, they'd been cursed with realistic fears about an apocalyptic future, but they refused to lose all hope. They were trying to figure out something that would make things better. And then, for both of them, something had gone very wrong.

Unless you aren't telling me everything, I said to Jacobi. Aren't you doing exactly what Lenin did during his exile in Europe? Honing your message, building a network, weighing tactical options, creating a mystique?

He smiled. "I wouldn't be a very good revolutionary if I told you I was doing that."

CHAPTER 13

BEST REGARDS, TED

As instructed, I gave Kaczynski the year he asked for and tried again. I asked for his thoughts on eco-fascism and the Mexican eco-terrorist group with the name that translates as "Individuals Tending to the Wild." I asked him about the youthful anti-civ movement and whether it was worthy of support even though it was leftist. Didn't a revolution need a restless population ready for change?

Wrong! "Thank you for your undated letter postmarked 6/11/18, but you wrote the address so sloppily I'm surprised that it reached me," he began. He wanted nothing to do with the anti-civ kids. They were feckless and unreliable. As to my tactical concerns:

> If you've read my *Anti-Tech Revolution* then you haven't understood it. You don't *have* to hold power. You don't *have* to destroy every single machine. All you have to do is disable some key components of the system so that the whole thing collapses. How long does it take to do that? A year? A month? A week?

He added a few more instructions. Contact his publisher for any background information I might need on his legal case, hire a big-name firm of high-powered lawyers to get into the prison for an interview—and don't ever mention ITS again. That could get him in trouble. "Hypothesis: ITS is instigated by some country's security services—probably Mexico," he wrote. "Their real task is to spread hopelessness, because where there is no hope there is no serious resistance."

Wait . . . Ted Kaczynski was hopeful? The Ted Kaczynski who wanted to destroy industrial civilization? The idea seemed ridiculous right up to the moment it spun around and became obvious. For the last twenty years, he'd been sending an unceasing stream of strategic advice in the essays and letters from his prison cell. He was hopeful civilization could be destroyed.

Then, as if he couldn't resist, he responded to my earlier question about America's partisan divides.

Present situation looks a lot like situation (19th century) leading up to the Russian Revolution, or (pre-1911) to Chinese Revolution. You have all these different factions, mostly goofy and unrealistic, and in disagreement if not in conflict with one another, but all agreeing that the situation is intolerable and that change of the most radical kind is necessary and inevitable. To this mix add one leader of genius.

Ah, that one leader of genius.

In my next letter, I asked if any candidates for that position had approached him. His answer was an impatient no—any revolutionary stupid enough to write to him would be too stupid to lead a revolution. Then he broke off mid-sentence. "Wait, I just thought of an exception: John Jacobi. But he's a screwball—bad judgment—unreliable—a problem rather than a help."

However, he wrote, if *I* came across any serious anti-tech people or groups, he'd appreciate a heads-up. He even gave me the name of someone to contact. "Failing that, will you send these individuals or groups the address of an anti-tech website that has been set up by a European friend of ours?"

And I could stop calling him "Dr. Kaczynski." "Ted" would be fine.

•

In the year I'd waited, 2017, Ted had become a bigger story. A magazine called *First Things* published an article called "Searching for Ted Kaczynski," which was notable because it was written by the deputy editor and because the magazine was home to influential old-school Christian conservatives like Richard John Neuhaus and William J. Bennett. "What I found in the text, and in letters written by Kaczynski since his incarceration," he said, "was a man with a large number of astute (even prophetic) insights into American political life and culture. Much of his thinking would be at home in the pages of First Things."

An eight-part dramatic series called *Manhunt: Unabomber* was a hit when it premiered on the Discovery Channel that year and a "super hit" when Netflix rereleased it later that year, a producer named Elliott Halpern told me. That's why Netflix had commissioned Halpern to make another film, this one focusing on Ted's ideas and legacy. "Obviously," Halpern said, "he predicted a lot of stuff." Ted's papers have become a top attraction at the University of Michigan's Labadie archive, one of the world's largest collections of original documents from movements of social unrest, the head archivist told me. Although they have a policy against characterizing the clientele, she defended Ted's readers. "Nobody seems crazy. I've heard a few of them say, 'His predictions are coming true.'"

In 2017, *Foreign Policy* published an article called "The Next Wave of Extremists Will Be Green." Written by an expert in radicalism and social media analysis named Jamie Bartlett, it claimed that a "few thousand" Americans were already prepared to break the law, citing examples like the Standing Rock protests along with evidence of online organizing. "The necessary conditions for the radicalization of climate activism are all in place. Some groups are already showing signs of making the transition."

But at that point, it was still mostly talk. Although the FBI wouldn't discuss the topic or even give an official statement, the 2017 report on domestic terrorism by the Congressional Research Service cited just a handful of minor attacks on "symbols of Western civilization" in the previous ten years, giving credit to Operation Backfire, the FBI crackdown that crushed Rod Coronado and the rest of the radical environmentalist movement in the mid-2000s. The pace wouldn't pick up until 2021, when the FBI reported a huge jump in people facing charges for crimes related to domestic terrorism, from 180 to 800. Although this was attributed mostly to the January 6, 2021, attack on Congress, it may be significant that the FBI attributed the surge to "an increase in anti-government or anti-authority violent extremism" (as the Congressional Research Service paraphrased it), a category that includes both anarchists and right-wing militias.

Attacks around that time included the shooting of a Republican member of Congress at a baseball game in 2017, sixteen undetonated mail bombs sent to Democrats and members of the media in 2018, the attack on Paul Pelosi in 2022 and at least six more violent attacks of lesser notoriety. Of the 2,700 investigations the FBI pursued between October 2021 and 2022, only 1 percent regarded animal rights or the environment: two anarchists in Missouri set fire to a convenience store during the Black Lives Matter protests, two more damaged construction equipment in Utah, ten people in masks shut down a pipeline in Michigan and an unknown number shot up a pipeline substation in South Dakota. Racial and ethnic attacks totaled 19 percent. But 70 percent were anti-some-kind-of-authority.

I was changing too. In my next letter, I told Ted how his comment about the necessity of hope affected me. "This may seem sentimental," I wrote, "but it's moving that someone who thought your thoughts and who's been through what you've been through could retain even a shred of that old American positive thinking. It's a good reminder not to wallow in the dark thoughts that come at 4:00 a.m."

●

Ted wrote again, asking me to help out a friend who was looking for a job. He started to give me a hard time, apparently teasing me. "Thank you for your letter of 8/6/18, which I received on 8/16/19. It looks like a more elaborate and better developed, but otherwise typical, example of the type of brown-nosing that journalists send to a 'mark' to get him to cooperate." He wrote something like that in almost every letter.

Whatever I ended up writing, he said, it would probably just reduce the anti-tech movement to another part of the spectacle "that keeps people entertained and therefore thoughtless."

Ouch. He had a point.

Writing to him became a challenge of its own, like trying to solve a puzzle. Over and over, he returned to his obsession: Anti-tech people need to learn how to mobilize and organize resistance. "The current political turmoil provides an environment in which a revolutionary movement should be able to gain a foothold and make a name for itself—if it goes about it the right way." S. M. Buehler's *Understanding Social Movements* would be a useful resource. Because this seemed like an implicit rejection of his long, solitary bombing campaign, I wanted to ask him why he'd shifted tactics, but I was holding off for a better time. Even so, he must have worried he'd gone too far. He mentioned a guy who wrote to him and then tried to blow up a gas pipeline. He couldn't correspond with people like that, he said. Same with Jacobi, who'd mentioned something in one of his letters about inciting people to acts of sabotage. "If you've been in contact with anyone who is or may become involved in illegal activities," Ted told me, "I don't want to hear about it."

But he did want to hear about it, he really did. And I had something I wanted to tell him.

CHAPTER 14

DARK ECOLOGISTS

A few days after Luigi was arrested, I got a notice about a new post on *Biocentric*, a blog I follow. Some bits:

> Fuck the New York Times, CNN, MSNBC, WSJ, Washington Post, Fox News, and all corporate media . . .

> Oh, the poor health insurers! Meanwhile, these companies are responsible for MURDER on the daily. They kill people just as directly and just as dead . . .

> Damn right we're angry. Poor people are being killed for money daily and it barely registers. We need to tear the goddamn corporate state to the ground.

> #LuigiMangione

The writer was Max Wilbert, one of the founders of a radical activist network called Deep Green Resistance. On paper, DGR meets most of Ted's requirements for a revolutionary organization. The original core group spent five years holding conferences and private meetings to build consensus and hone a message, then publicized it effectively with a book by the same name, which begins with the premise that "civilization is killing the planet" and frames its tactical options as speculations: "If selective disruption doesn't work soon enough, some resisters may conclude that all-out-disruption is needed to keep the planet from burning to a cinder" and launch "coordinated actions on a large scale" against the vital organs of the system. Assassinations were a possibility too, purely speculative, of course.

By the end of the group's first year in existence, 2012, DGR had nearly two hundred members. Six years later, it had nearly 150,000 people following it online. Jacobi said they were hobbled by a doctrinal war over TERFs, an acronym for "trans-exclusionary radical feminists," so they were rallying the troops with a crash course in resistance training at a secret retreat near Yellowstone National Park. "This training is aimed at activists who are tired of ineffective actions," the promotional flyer read. "Topics will include hard and soft blockades, hit and run tactics, police interactions, legal repercussions, operational security, terrain advantages and more."

I signed up for the secret resistance training and flew out to Montana at the end of June 2018. My phone pinged at the Avis counter in Bozeman. A guy named Matt needed a ride. I found him standing outside. He was in his early thirties, dressed in conventional clothes, short hair, no visible tattoos, the kind of person the organizers of a militant resistance group might send to check out a visitor from the media. When we got on the road and had a chance to talk, he said he was a middle school social studies teacher. He was sympathetic to the urge to attack critical infrastructure, but he'd prefer to destroy civilization by legal means, possibly by a gradual "decoupling" from the modern world through radical restrictions on the use of technology, town by town and state by state.

But if that was true, why was he here?

"See for yourself," he said.

We reached the camp in the late afternoon and set up our tents. A purple mountain rose behind us, another purple mountain stood ahead, a deep blue lake filled the canyon below. I remembered Jacobi's words, "Nature is the only place where you feel awe." The group gathered an hour later in a big yurt with a plywood floor, sofas and folding chairs: one student activist from UC Irvine, two Native American veterans of the Standing Rock pipeline protests, three radical lawyers, a shy working-class kid from Mississippi, a former abortion clinic volunteer and a few people who didn't want to be identified or quoted in any way. The session started with a warning about loose lips and a lecture on DGR's "non-negotiable guidelines" for men—hold back, listen, agree or disagree respect-fully, avoid male-centered words, follow the lead of women.

The first speaker was Sakej Ward, a former soldier who'd done a tour of Afghanistan with the U.S. Airborne and then a few more years in the Canadian military. He was a member of both the Wolf Clan of British Columbia and the Mi'kmaq of northern Maine, had two degrees in political science, impressive muscles bulging through a T-shirt from some karate club and one of those flat, wide Mohawks you see on outlaw bikers. Unfortunately, he put his entire presentation off the record, so all I can tell you is that the theme was Native American warrior societies.

Later, Ward told me that the warrior societies died out with the buffalo and the open range. They sprouted a few leaves in the 1980s, died again when the FBI cracked down on radical environmentalists with Operation Bite Back, then sprouted again after the crash of 2008. Now more and more young men were holding training sessions in the woods and learning the old ways that kept people rooted in nature. They were also starting to reconnect with radical environmentalists at events like the Standing Rock protests in 2016. "It's a question of 'Are they there yet?'" he said. "We've been fighting this war for five hundred years. But climate change is creating an atmosphere where it can happen."

For the next two days, our courses ranged from computer security to old activist techniques like using "lockboxes" to chain yourself to bulldozers and fences, the last given almost apologetically, like a class in 1950s home cooking. In another session, Ward took a group of trainees into the forest and lined us up single file. Imagine you're on a military patrol, he said, turning his back to lead the way. We marched. Suddenly, he shot his left arm out to the side, elbow bent to ninety degrees, palm facing us. "Freeze," he barked.

We froze.

"That's the best way to conceal yourself from the enemy," he told us. Motion catches the eye; frozen in place, we might blend into the leaves.

He showed us more hand signs. For enemy, you make a pistol with your hand and turn it thumbs down. Danger is a diagonal slash.

After eight or ten examples, he stopped. "Why am I making all the signs with my left hand?"

No one knew.

He turned around to face us with his finger pointed down the barrel of an invisible gun. "Because you always have to have a finger in control of your weapon," he said.

The other trainees were pumped afterward. "You can take out transformers with a fifty-caliber," one man said.

"But you don't just want to do one," said another. "You want four-man teams taking out ten transformers. That would bring the whole system to a halt."

Ted would have been fairly pleased with this so far, I thought. Ward was certainly a plausible contender for the Lenin role. So was Max Wilbert, the veteran DGR organizer running the event, with his Mephistophelian beard and quietly watchful manner. "We talk about 'cascading catastrophic effects,'" he told us in one of the last yurt meetings, summing up DGR's grand strategy. "A large percent of the world's oil supply is processed in an oil facility in Louisiana, for example. If that was taken down, it would have cascading effects all over the world."

But then Matt and an amiable engineer from Denver committed micro-aggressions, causing the DGR women to gather everyone in the yurt for a lecture on patriarchy, which had to be destroyed at the same time as civilization. Otherwise, what's the point? Also, men who are voluntarily assuming gendered aspects of female identity should never be allowed in female-sovereign spaces. And don't use the expression "TERF" unless you want another lecture on micro-aggression.

Matt listened to all this from the back of the crowd. Wearing a hoodie and mirrored glasses, he looked exactly like the famous police sketch of the Unabomber in a hoodie and mirrored glasses. I'm pretty sure he was trolling the women at the podium. And why not? They were doing exactly what Ted had told us those feckless leftists would do, which is get distracted by secondary pursuits.

At the farewell dinner, one of the more mysterious trainees finally spoke up. With long, wild hair, a floppy wilderness hat, pants tucked into waterproof boots, a wary expression and an actual cabin in Montana, he projected the mad hermit vibe with impressive authenticity. He was involved in some risky stuff during the Cove-Mallard logging protests in Idaho back in the 1990s, he said, and went into hiding after the FBI brought him in for questioning. But lately he'd been getting the feeling that things were starting to change, and now he was sure of it. "I've been in a coma for twenty years," he said. "I want to thank you guys for being here when I woke up." One of the radical lawyers wrapped up with a lyrical tribute to Thomas MacDonagh, the schoolteacher who led the Dublin brigade in Ireland's legendary 1916 rebellion and whistled as he was led to the firing squad.

On the drive back to the airport, I asked Matt if he was really a middle school teacher. He answered with a question: "What is your real interest in this thing?"

I mentioned John Jacobi.

"I know him," Matt said. "We've traded a few emails."

Of course they did. Matt was another serious young man with gears turning behind his eyes, sending his probes into the vast, twitching nervous system of the internet, dreaming of cascading effects.

"Can you imagine actually doing something like that?" I asked. After Max's last lecture about the oil facility in Louisiana, I didn't have to say what.

"Well," he answered, drawing out the pause. "Thomas Mac-Donagh was a schoolteacher."

I checked in on Matt a few months later, and he sent me some things he'd been writing on his blog:

A system that murders the powerless and steals the wealth of the world must go down so hard it can't come back up EVER AGAIN. This requires a two-step process: 1. Cut supply lines [trains/rails, trucks/roads, ships/ports . . .] that transport goods and raw materials. 2. Cripple key nodes of industrial infrastructure responsible for catastrophic ecological collapse.

•

After reading his post about Luigi, I contacted Max Wilbert. We'd been in touch a few times since the training session, so I knew he'd quit DGR a few years before and pitched his tent with indigenous protesters at the Thacker Pass lithium mine in Nevada for most of a year, which got him slapped with a lawsuit from the mining company. I wasn't sure I supported this cause any more than I did animal rights back in the days of Zach Fredell and Rod Coronado—we need lithium for electric cars, don't we?—but I admired his commitment, so I kicked in a hundred bucks to help with legal fees. These days, he said, he was getting a master's degree in "degrowth," a new specialty in peaceful strategies for deindustrialization. It sounded like the same thing Matt had called "decoupling" after the DGR retreat, almost seven years ago now. Long enough for it to have become an academic field.

I read your Luigi post, I said. I want to ask you how you keep from killing people.

Max laughed and gave me the responsible answer: DGR's official positions are in the DGR book, also called *Deep Green Resistance*, and the DGR book wasn't really in favor of direct violence against individuals. He doesn't speak for them officially anymore, but even sections about the righteousness of attacks on refineries and turbines framed their arguments as mere speculation, he said. Then he immediately hedged it. "To what extent that was determined by the extensive legal review that that book had to go through before it was published, I don't know, because I wasn't one of the authors."

Max's dad was in the military, but his grandfather was a Quaker and a conscientious objector, so he split the difference—he thought of himself as peaceful, he said, but not a pacifist. "There are absolutely circumstances in which not only is violence justified, but it's essential and it's righteous."

Luigi's alleged deed, for example. A lot of people view it from the perspective of poor Brian Thompson, just a random family man gunned down in the street in a senseless attack. But there's a different way of looking at it, Max said. Think of Brian Thompson as the administrator of a concentration camp. "He's not holding the guns. He's not pressing the buttons in the gas chambers. He's not directly killing anyone. But he is facilitating an administrative process by which thousands of people are being condemned to death."

Max ran DGR's field operations for fifteen years. In that time, I asked him, how many people had he met who could do something like that?

"Expand on the parameters of your question," he said.

"Well, just, you know, use violence to spark something."

"Not that many," he answered. "At least not that many who made it clear to me."

Then he continued, this time without any prompting. "But if you're talking about people who are supportive of that type of action, and I could see as potentially doing something like that, theoretically, not telling me 'I want to' or 'I'm going to,' then over fifteen years and all the events and talks and meetings and trainings, probably dozens, if not the low hundreds."

In February 2024, a Cambridge professor named Sean Fleming did a forensic analysis of the Peaceful Environmentalist theory, which states that environmental activists do not kill people. They'll set a ski resort on fire or blow up a pipeline, but their belief that life is sacred makes bloodshed awkward. After going through all the possibilities, Fleming found that the Peaceful Environmentalist theory was in fact one of the strongest theories in contemporary political science. "A few radical environmentalist groups, such as Deep Green Resistance, have argued that lethal violence is justified and even necessary to prevent a global ecological catastrophe," he said, "but none, so far, seem to have followed through on their bellicose rhetoric."

The one exception was Ted Kaczynski, and Fleming didn't think he was really an environmentalist. He'd gone through the arguments for insanity and revenge and arrived at the conclusion that Ted's obsession with "wild nature" was his biggest motive, but that *wild* was the dominant term. What Kaczynski really wanted was personal freedom. He hated the idea of being another cog in the machine. So I wasn't surprised when Max said that his trainees avoided talk of violence. Either they were basically peaceful leftists at heart, just like Ted said, or they were smart enough to keep it to themselves.

Was Luigi justified? I asked him.

"Based on what appears to be known about his motivations, yeah, probably," Max said.

Does that make Luigi the secret ideal of DGR? If he did it? The guy who went out there and took violent action that will maybe create some kind of chain effect?

"I don't know," Max said. "It's too early to tell."

But he seemed hopeful.

CHAPTER 15

FAN MAIL

In March 2025, after three months behind bars, Luigi made a chart to show people he'd received their letters, using their initials and the last two letters of their zip codes to keep them anonymous. I have to admit, it was a bit of a thrill to see "JR-24" there.

Some of his letters were starting to hit the media too. In one, he responded to a woman named Karen who wrote about her daughter's struggle with a rare disease and UnitedHealthcare's denials, which seemed to have been AI driven. The daughter fell into a coma before treatment was finally approved by order of a state insurance board. At that point, Karen saw the TV footage of Luigi's perp walk, a moment she later described to journalist Ashley Shelby: "I saw that the ruling class was absolutely terrified of us, and that sent a bolt of energy through me like nothing ever has (except maybe motherhood)." So Karen dashed off a letter, including a photocopy of the *Christ in Majesty* mosaic in Washington, DC, a striking image of a fierce, muscular Jesus.

Shelby printed a screenshot of the letter Luigi wrote Karen in response: "Your letter is the first to make me tear up. I am so, so sorry for what you and your daughter so senselessly had to endure."

After giving her instructions on how to send photographs, he continued: "If you are able to send a photo of you/your daughter or the mosaic, it would mean a great deal to me. I will put it up on my prison cell wall next to your letter."

He added one more line, guaranteed to stir his supporters. "Your daughter is blessed to have a mother who loves her so much and fights for her so relentlessly." Isn't that what he'd done, fight for us relentlessly? So relentlessly that he might face the death penalty?

Another Luigi letter surfaced on Reddit, this one to a woman named Genevieve. "It's interesting to hear that you're majoring in nursing, and I hope your courses are going well." He gave some glimpses of his day, which consisted of "reading, eating lots of ramen, exercising, and spending time with my fellow brothers here," which is an awfully friendly word to use, with associations of solidarity and struggle. "We have chess nights on Wednesdays, and it's a fun way to pass time together." He recommended one of the books he read as a freshman at UPenn, *Self-Compassion: The Proven Power of Being Kind to Yourself*, and told her it had been a great source of support to him. But the most characteristic note was another pat on the back: "I understand the feeling of wanting to give up at times. Navigating young adulthood can be tough, but I believe we can all find our way through. I wish you best of luck with your graduation next semester. You have a bright future ahead."

Another Luigi letter showed up on Threads, this one a grateful appreciation of a fan's analysis of *The Lorax*: "I have thought many times that *The Lorax* is an almost foundational lesson, on par with many of Aesop's fables, that it will be so critical to read to my kids."

Others keep surfacing, mostly just details about his day or comments on shared interests. He was listening to the Agni Kai music from the soundtrack to *Avatar: The Last Airbender*. His favorite movie scene was the Battle of Carthage reenactment in *Gladiator*. He tried to ease one correspondent's anxieties about his well-being. "Please don't worry about my circumstances. It's fine here. I am very low maintenance, and most importantly humans are born resilient." There's that nurturing tone again. The odd part is how continuous it is with the nurturing tone he expressed before the shooting, as if he became another person in the months when he dropped out of sight—an arrogant young man who could say he was the first person to face the question of corporate greed "with such ruthless honesty" when *his own reading list* showed he knew better. In the urgency of those last months, even his spelling and grammar got worse. Then he reverted right back to Kind Luigi as soon as he got to prison.

On his legal information page, one line he wrote jumps out: "Powerfully, this support has transcended political, racial, and even class divisions, as mail has flooded MDC from across the country, and around the globe." It's that high-rung vision again, the Tim Urban dream. Luigi was trying to gather a community—and succeeding. His fundraising committee hit its $700,000 goal in March, with one person contributing $30,000 and another $36,500. In May, it reached its million-dollar goal, and the target was raised to $1.5 million. Social media sites like X and Bluesky were peppered with feeds named "Account that just posts Luigi Mangione" or "The Luigi Nicholas Mangione Community Page." His popularity on Reddit led to an unprecedented wave of censorship, with supportive subreddits repeatedly shut down by the administrators. In some cases, people have been flagged for violence just for upvoting posts that mention his first name. The r/FreeLuigi subreddit has managed to stay alive, with nearly forty thousand members at last count, by banning the use of the phrase "Delay Deny Depose" along with any support of violence—and any sexualization of Luigi, heaven forbid. The moderators even told members to refer to Luigi as "LM" to dodge the algorithm. Some started calling him "Mario's brother."

The courthouse crowd exploded, too, going from a few dozen at the December hearing to at least a hundred people packing the hallway in February and hundreds more outside. Mostly women, it is true, but not all young or goo-goo eyed—he seems to have gathered a substantial motherly contingent, too.

Lauren Davidson-Ibarra, for example, a married lawyer from California who helped me get oriented when I arrived, said she was worried about Luigi's relationship with his family and conditions in the prison. She first got interested in the case because of all the "thoughts and prayers out of network" jokes that burst out online after the shooting, "like something that had been sparked." She also found the arrest suspicious—if he was smart enough to have planned the perfect crime, why was he sitting in a McDonald's with all the evidence on him?

And let's face it, his looks didn't hurt. As she put it on her Substack:

Imagine that I'm placing my hands on your shoulders and looking deeply into your eyes, the fate of the world and all of humankind depending on what I'm about to tell you . . . take a deep breath . . . and hear me: *He is even more handsome in person!* I know this may be difficult to believe or accept for some, but I assure you that it is the truth. To quote Jesus, "He that hath ears to hear, let him hear!" Luigi Mangione is More. Handsome. In. Person. His hair had grown longer and even more luxurious. His brows were the brows of the Roman Gods of his ancestors. He was taller than both of the guards who held each of his arms, he has to be at least 6'1". His jawline, 5 o'clock shadow, and lips, were out of a Caravaggio painting.

Ibarra flew out early and went to the court building the day before the hearing to check things out, but none of the guards and clerks had any information about how she could get a seat. She ended up paying someone to stand in line for her. Her stand-in arrived at 3:30 a.m. and got the fifth place in the line. Forty people were there when Lauren got there at 7:30, and the hearing wasn't starting for another seven hours. But she had an entertaining time fending off line-cutters and getting to know people. One woman showed off a tattoo of a flower with "Deny, Depose, and Defend" written on the petals, which prompted others to show off their own Luigi tattoos. A group of them were wearing green because the character named Luigi in the *Mario Kart* video game wears green—and then Luigi arrived in a Lincoln green sweater, sending his fans into peals of delight.

The chief guard walked up the aisle, hushing us. "No interviews in the hallway!" Why he cared I have no idea, but he seemed personally offended. As a reporter put it later in The Verge, the packed hallway felt like "a club with a strict bouncer."

Just before two, the elevator doors opened, cameras started flashing and the crowd stirred. The ones in front started to applaud when they saw Luigi's attorney, Karen Friedman Agnifilo. Cheers burst out. Agnifilo smiled, slowing down just a little bit to take it in. The head guard barked at her. "Counsel, have some respect. This is a courtroom!" When she moved on, he barked at the people in line. "If that happens again, I will clear this entire floor, and not a single person will get inside! Show some respect! Have some decorum!"

Once again, they brought Luigi down the hall chained hand and foot, which was objectively ridiculous. The courtroom was up on the fifteenth floor of a heavily guarded building, with another dozen guards standing on the sidelines of the room. They surrounded Luigi as if he were Bruce Banner about to turn green and burst free. But they also had him in a bulletproof vest this time, so maybe they were being pouty about having been criticized for neglecting his safety before. Or they were just jealous of his youth and beauty, given that they were mostly pasty, overweight middle-aged white men who looked like trolls with axes guarding an elfin prince. Agnifilo asked the judge to take off Luigi's chains, but the guards objected. After a sidebar, the judge said they wanted to keep him chained up "for security reasons."

But this cast a shadow on Luigi's presumption of innocence, Agnifilo said in response. He was a model prisoner, he hadn't given the police a single problem, all these guards were standing around—why couldn't they take off his chains? The judge shrugged it off. There was no jury present, so his presumption of innocence was irrelevant. But the result was, as Ibarra put it on her Substack later, "one of the most iconic photos of American legal and pop cultural history"—Luigi's bare ankles crossed under the table, cuffed and chained above those brown penny loafers.

Like the perp walk, the chains were just another overreaction that ended up glorifying him. This was starting to seem like a compulsion. Agnifilo told the judge she was shocked to see the New York City mayor and chief of detectives talking about the case in an HBO documentary—they had time to put on makeup and sit down for lengthy interviews about evidence she hadn't even seen? They hadn't turned over a single detective's report. They gave her footage from only one body cam. "This journal that they're calling his 'manifesto,'" she said, "we have never been provided copies."

Another odd thing: The state prosecutors secured an indictment back in December, but three months later, the federal prosecutors hadn't even brought the case to a grand jury. Everyone knew they were deciding whether to go for the death penalty.

Chants of "Free Luigi" rose from the sidewalk fifteen stories below.

The judge cut Agnifilo off. The state prosecutors were promising to provide all the discovery material within two weeks. He wanted the first pre-trial motions filed by April 9 and a hearing on June 26. If a problem developed with the discovery materials, Agnifilo could file supplementary motions later.

Outside, hundreds of protesters stood on the sidewalk with FREE LUIGI signs. Most of them were there for the health care theme, but the innocent-until-proven-guilty contingent was strong, and someone with a class war spirit had glued a few of those insurance executive Wanted posters to a fence. Two big LED panel trucks drove by flashing signs that said HEALTH CARE IS A HUMAN RIGHT, NO MORE DEATHS BY DENIALS and JURY

NULLIFICATION. They were financed by a new pop-up activist group called People over Profit NYC, which describes itself as "a movement rallying for healthcare reform and justice for Luigi Mangione." A woman named Taylor stood by their table with a green FREE LUIGI sign. "I pay taxes," she said, "and the fact that they used my tax money to pay for a Broadway entrance—" She stopped, shaking her head in disgust, then finished her thought: "But what do you expect when the government is controlled by lobbies, with billions and billions of dollars at stake?"

Another LED truck rolled by, this one using the Saint Luigi image to hawk a Luigi cryptocurrency created by an anonymous speculator. It shot up to $60 million the day after Luigi's arrest; six months later its market value was around $1.4 million. The speculator must be praying for the death penalty—how great that would be for the Saint Luigi business!

•

I also reached out to Sam Bush, one of the organizers of the December 4th Legal Committee fundraising campaign. He's thirty and a longtime activist who put in time at the Ferguson and Standing Rock protests. To Bush, the shooting was definitely a political assassination, "the targeted assassination of a private health insurance executive who has stood out in his field for developing cutting-edge mechanisms to deny claims, causing thousands and thousands of lives to be lost." A good thing, as far as he was concerned.

The fund was started by about fifteen normal people who'd been traumatized by claims denials, he said. This was two days after the shooting, before Luigi's hostel picture was released. They felt like "whoever took this bold, brazen, and unique act down in Manhattan was doing so essentially on their behalf, and they felt sort of indebted to someone who would sacrifice their life for a cause."

Bush continued, turning talking points into incantations: We're at a point in the human story when we don't have the luxury to be silent any longer, he said. Everything's falling apart, and everybody knows it. We're being moved toward a fascist government. People are profiting from the systematic destruction of our planet. So when somebody acts with such pointed clarity, millions of people are like, "Hell yeah, brother." That's especially true for a brother who had made such a valiant effort to avoid harming bystanders. "It was precise, and it was intentional, and that was at its core an act that has the capacity to change the world." As for any moral qualms about using violence to achieve progressive social change, Bush shrugged them off with a tone of weary disgust. "I've been raised in a world of violence. This entire world is oversaturated with galloping misery and ultra-violence." So sure, it's a tragedy when someone has their life unexpectedly cut short, and that is why *millions of Americans understand UnitedHealthcare as the actual violent actor.*

One month later, paranoia was rising among Luigi fans. With the Trump administration disappearing people into foreign prison camps, they were starting to worry about the dangers of sending Luigi posts or even *liking* Luigi posts. Forget getting banned on Reddit—would they end up on some kind of list? But they swore it wouldn't stop them.

CHAPTER 16

GOING FULL LUIGI

At the last minute, Abe Cabrera changed our rendezvous point from a restaurant in New Orleans to an alligator-filled swamp an hour away.

This wasn't a surprise.

Jacobi gave me Cabrera's email address, identifying him as the North American contact for ITS, the Mexican eco-terrorist group. Cabrera immediately denied this. His interest in ITS was purely academic, he said, an outgrowth of his studies in theology and the post-Hegelians. "However," he added, "to say that I don't have any contact with them may or may not be true."

Now he was leading me into a swamp, literally, talking about an ITS bomb attack on the head of the Department of Physical and Mathematical Sciences at the University of Chile in 2016. "Is that a fair target?" he asked. "For Uncle Ted, it would have been, so I guess that's the standard." He chuckled.

He was short, round, bald, full of nervous energy, wild theories and awkward tics—if Terrorist Spokesman didn't work out for him, he was a shoo-in for Mad Scientist in a B movie. Giant ferns and carpets of moss appeared and disappeared as he led the way into the darkness of the deep swamp.

He started checking out ITS after he heard some rumors about a new cell starting up in Torreón, his grandparents' birthplace in Mexico. But that version of ITS didn't catch his interest until the group changed its name to Wild Reaction. Why? Because healthy animals don't have "tendencies" when they confront an enemy. As one of the Wild Reaction members put it in a post-attack communiqué written in the purple prose poetry that became the group's signature: "I place the device, and it transforms me into a coyote thirsting for revenge."

Cabrera called this "radical animism," a phrase that conjures the specter of nature itself rising up in revolt. Somehow that notion wove together all the dizzying twists and turns he'd taken—the years as the child of migrant laborers in the vegetable fields of California's Imperial Valley, his flirtation with "super-duper Marxism" at the Berkeley campus of the University of California, a leap of faith that put him in an "ultraconservative, ultra-Catholic" monastery, the loss of faith that surprised him at the birth of his child. "Most people say, 'I held my kid for the first time and I realized God exists.' I held my kid the first time and I said, 'You know what? God is bullshit.'"

Surprised, I asked him to explain. He said the beautiful little girl cradled in his arms would just grow up to join the eight billion people who were already destroying the world. She could be the best person ever, and it wouldn't matter. His daughter would be a force of destruction. People were great in small doses but deadly in large ones, end of story. Good, evil, whatever. If that was God's plan, the whole thing was about as spiritually meaningful as a marshmallow.

John Jacobi was a big part of this story, he added. A search for examples of radical animism led him to one of Jacobi's websites, *Hunter/Gatherer*. The two began sharing ideas about ITS and Ùltimo Reducto. They both contributed to *Atassa*, a magazine openly dedicated, right on the first page, to the premise that "civilization should be fought and the example of Ted Kaczynski is what that fighting looks like." Both wrote essays for *Attasa*'s premier edition, in fact, but Jacobi made the prudent decision to write in a detached and scholarly tone. Cabrera's prose slogged along in turgid scholarship before breaking free with a flourish of familiar prose poetry: "A wild animal may flee, but when cornered, it does not roll over and obey, it attacks."

Cabrera wove in and out of corners like a prisoner looking for an escape route, so it was hard to know why he chose a magazine reporter for his most incendiary confession: "Here's the super-official version I haven't told anybody—*I am the unofficial voice-slash-theoretician of eco-extremism.* I translated all thirty communiqués. I translated one last night."

Abe Cabrera: Abracadabra.

Yes, he knew this put him dangerously close to violating the laws against material contributions to terrorism. He'd read the USA PATRIOT Act. That's why he led a double life, even a triple life. Nobody at work knew, nobody from in his past knew, even his wife didn't know. He certainly didn't want his kids to know. He didn't even want to tell them about climate change. Math homework, piano lessons, gymnastics lessons—he was knee-deep in all that stuff. He punched the clock. "What else am I gonna do?" he asked. "I love my kids. I hope for their future even though they have no future."

His mood sank, reminding me of John Jacobi. Abrupt shifts in perspective seemed to be part of their world.

Puma hunted here before the Europeans came, Cabrera said,

staring into the swamp. Bears and alligators too, things that could kill you. The cypress trees used to be three times as thick. When you looked around now, you saw how much everything had suffered. But he still couldn't shake the lingering sense that there was something greater out there. As Saint Thomas Aquinas said, sort of, "What may not be visible to the eye of the bat may be visible to the eye of the eagle."

Cabrera chuckled. What can you do? Your mind shuts down, you want to lash out with that wild reaction. "It's like, be the psychopathic destruction you want to see in the world," he said, peering off into the mossy shadows where no puma roamed.

●

Cabrera dropped out of sight a few months after that day in the swamp. He'd been doxed online by an anarchist who was angry about his support for violence, which made the peaceful anarchists of today look bad. This exposed Cabrera's secrets to his family and the company that employed him, destroying his life as it was. I've tried to contact him on the old secure channels, without success.

And Zach Fredell? Paul Kingsnorth? John Jacobi?

A few months after my visit with Jacobi at the modern Stone Age village of Wild Roots, I caught up with him on the phone. He was back in Chapel Hill and feeling shaky, he said. He kept screwing up. He'd let people down. He was starting to consider the possibility that his troubled past may have affected his judgment. He still believed in the revolution, but honestly, he wasn't sure what he'd do if somebody gave him a magic bottle of Civ-Away. He'd probably use it. Or maybe not.

Six months later, he was working in a fish store and thinking of going back to school. Maybe he could get a job in forest conservation. He wanted to have a kid someday. He brought up Paul Kingsnorth. "I'm coming to terms with the fact that it might very well be true that there's not much you can do, but I'm having a real hard time just letting go with a hopeless sigh."

But Jacobi was lost in his mind a lot, hard to reach. He'd find a place to stay and then drift off again. Last I heard, he was sleeping rough on the outskirts of Chapel Hill. I walked some of the homeless camps with his picture and people said yeah, they'd seen him, maybe.

In 2020, Kingsnorth realized there was a void inside him that "turned out to be God-shaped" and took the leap of faith into the very traditional Romanian Orthodox Church. This did nothing to endear him to his critics on the left, who had escalated their criticisms with labels like "nationalist," "heteronormative" and "neocolonial." But to Rod Dreher, a prominent religious conservative who'd written *The Benedict Option*, a book calling for Christians to withdraw from secular society and form their own communities, Kingsnorth became nothing less than a prophet "rethinking Christianity in a new way that's returning it to its ancient roots." Dreher even joined Kingsnorth at a lecture in England called "Resisting the Machine," with Dreher promoting a new book (*Living in Wonder: Finding Mystery and Meaning in a Secular Age*) that devoted most of a chapter to the dark enchantments of AI.

If there was ever a sign of the impending apocalypse, those two teaming up must be it.

And Zach Fredell, my first exposure to the Uncle Ted generation? He almost went full Luigi on some abusive Mexican soldiers around 2008, but he stopped himself because he knew they'd end up taking their revenge on the village he was visiting. Somehow that got him into working with a Lions Club from Phoenix to distribute five thousand pairs of eyeglasses to the Huichol indigenous tribe, which led to five years of support work. He bailed on the green radicals because of "the whole LGBTQ dogma" that started to take over in the early 2000s. Not that he cares what people do, he said, but what kind of idiot goes out to a reservation to give lectures on gender to indigenous people who are looking for allies against *the beast that's been devouring them alive since Columbus*?

After that, he focused on opposing the Iraq War. He joined a "black bloc" group of radical protesters who wear black clothing and face masks to commit acts of sabotage and took a Molotov cocktail to a protest in Denver. The police helicopters made him too paranoid to throw it, but the Joint Terrorism Task Force took an interest in him anyway and even went to his dad's house looking for him, so he hit the road and ended up in Morocco, where he married a woman from the Berber indigenous people, had a couple of kids and started a small biodiesel business. Life happens. But he still thinks Ted was right—melt a few more icebergs into the North Atlantic Current, and it's going to be *The Day After Tomorrow* for real, he told me. In fact, he posted "Ted Lives!" online recently and someone brought up the computer store owner Ted killed, Hugh Scrutton, who was just a random guy running his little shop. Zach had zero sympathy. "When colonization started in North America, was the guy who sold the bullets just the shop owner?"

He can't say anything more. There's a U.S. listening station a kilometer away. In fact, he wants to make one thing very clear—he has no intention of hurting anyone, especially not in Morocco.

CHAPTER 17

COUNTDOWN

On January 23, 2024, eleven months before the shooting, Luigi launched a document dump. He started with his review of Ted's manifesto, singling out four quotes. The famous opening and the passage about over-socialization were obvious choices, but he also chose two that seem more personal. The first was a line about mental health as a measure of how well a person adjusts to the system without showing signs of stress. The other was a sentence about conservatives being fools because they whine about the decay of traditional values while supporting economic growth: "Apparently it never occurs to them that you can't make rapid, drastic changes in the technology and the economy of a society without causing rapid changes in all other aspects of the society as well."

His choice of that passage marked a change. Luigi's belief in technology seemed to have dimmed, which must have played a role in his decision to blow off his six-figure job at TrueCar. He was also more explicit in criticizing conservative thinking, which could indicate that he was moving past the anti-woke stuff.

January 23 was also the day he posted his rave review of

What's Our Problem? And he revisited *How to Break Up with Your Phone: The 30-Day Plan to Take Back Your Life*, which he'd first commented on way back in 2020. "This little book packs a punch," he said, linking to his own summaries of each chapter: "The goal is not to throw your phone under a bus. Smartphones are amazing tools . . ."

He gave five stars to Steve Stewart-Williams's *The Ape That Understood the Universe*, a book about psychological and cultural evolution.

He gave five stars to Yuval Noah Harari's high-rung look at evolution and the future, *Sapiens: A Brief History of Humankind*, singling out some very Ted-like quotes: "We did not domesticate wheat. It domesticated us." Also, "The romantic contrast between modern industry that 'destroys nature' and our ancestors who 'lived in harmony with nature' is groundless. Long before the Industrial Revolution, *Homo sapiens* held the record among all organisms for driving the most plant and animal species to their extinctions." And a quote about all the young folks who think they'll get a high-paying job and quit in their thirties to follow their dreams, but when their thirties arrive they're stuck with mortgages and kids.

Also on that same day, he gave four stars to *Can't Hurt Me*, a book on how to "master your mind and defy the odds" that was recommended by Joe Rogan. Written by David Goggins, the Army/Navy/Air Force triple threat whose work Luigi followed, it focuses on Goggins's personal story of rising above the traumas of racism and physical abuse through ferocious physical discipline. Luigi called it "extreme" but also "good fuel to kickstart your system out of a rut." He added an odd warning: "Eventual balance must be achieved though after the initial crisis has been handled."

The initial crisis? Is he talking about his back surgery or something else?

On the next day, January 24, Luigi asked for responses to a quote from an Indian writer named Jiddu Krishnamurti, "It is no measure of health to be well adjusted to a profoundly sick society," a slight variation on the lines about mental health in Ted's manifesto. He also posted a response from someone named Neil Harrigan, who said society is what really needs to change. Three days later, Luigi put *The Lorax* on his reading list, singling out that quote about nothing changing unless someone cares an awful lot.

But on the twenty-fourth, he also posted a three-part thread about how he used to get bummed in math class because all the low-hanging scientific breakthroughs had been made in ancient Greece, but now he feels lucky because he can just download all that stuff and focus on the topics the twenty-first-century mind should explore. Which seems awfully optimistic for someone who thinks he's living in a profoundly sick society.

Another post the next day quoted Urban about how smart people are more prone to confirmation bias because "confirmation bias is what happens when the little lawyer in your head takes control of your thinking process—and smart people have a very smart little lawyer in there." What was that smart little lawyer saying to Luigi?

In other comments, he defended psychedelic mushrooms and weed and gave what seems to be an ironic response to a right-wing account griping about porn. "Porn should be regulated no less than alcohol, cigarettes, and travel." He gave Orwell's *1984* four stars, same as the Unabomber Manifesto. He posted a Goodreads review of Urban's worshipful five-part *Wait But Why* series on

Elon Musk, giving it five stars. But he marked it "read" way back in 2018. Was this a message too? Why the sudden flurry of posts?

Over the following months, Luigi kept on giving advice on back pain and having normal conversations about ordinary things. When a guy named Johnny Brown posted a list of his workout tips, Luigi gushed. "These are phenomenal. Took me years to learn on my own." Brown responded with a "thanks brother," and Luigi responded with a reference to a high-end brand of protein and vitamin supplements. "Just saw that you are a Legion athlete. Makes sense!" Once again hitting that encouraging note.

He kept putting books on his reading list too. He wanted to read more serious literature, like *Moby-Dick*, *Catch-22*, *Siddhartha* and *Walden*. Other additions were more in line with Tim Urban's last-page-of-humanity drawings, like a book by Sir Martin Rees, Britain's royal astronomer, called *Our Final Hour: A Scientist's Warning: How Terror, Error, and Environmental Disaster Threaten Humankind's Future in This Century—on Earth and Beyond*. He also added Jacques Ellul's prophetic book on the spiritual and social dangers of technology, *The Technological Society*. And this pertinent title: *Helplessness: On Depression, Development, and Death*.

He flew to Japan in February 2024. Online, he wrote a post about taking along no more than he could get into a single backpack, the ultimate minimalist lifestyle.

From *Brave New World*, he singled out this quote: "I don't want comfort. I want God, I want poetry, I want real danger, I want freedom, I want goodness. I want sin."

He also put *Atlas Shrugged* and *Mein Kampf* on his reading list around this time.

This is when he started to get interested in Jash Dholani, a popular X poster who'd been retweeted by manosphere celebrities like Jordan Peterson and Elon Musk. Luigi had put Dholani on one of his "follow" lists a couple of years earlier but didn't interact with him then. His first comment about a link from Dholani was an "essential read to understand modern civilization," but the link was dead by the time of his arrest, and nobody's been able to figure out what the link led to. On March 21, he reposted Dholani's mash note to Elon Musk, who'd just announced that he was "in a battle to the death with the anti-civilizational woke mind virus." Dholani said he admired Musk's commitment to saving humanity but asked him to remember the real enemy, the dream of equality. "The levelers want to destroy everything because in the rubble we will all be equal."

Luigi left no comment on this, but a few days later, he reposted Tim Urban saying he hoped all parents would keep kids under sixteen from using social media. The contrast is striking. Concern for troubled young people feels much more Luigi than Dholani's fanboy version of Ayn Rand, but Luigi loved the idea of being a high-rung thinker as much as he hated the thought of being an NPC, and with all those right-leaning strains in his family, he must have marinated in conservative confirmation bias throughout his childhood. Put all that together and what a fish with feathers you get—a kindhearted, deep-thinking, tech bro–adjacent, woke-mind-virus social justice warrior.

Is that even possible?

•

On April 1, Luigi began a revealing series of exchanges on X with a trollish but thoughtful guy going by the online handle "Max, gay and retarded moron." Max asked why so many people on the internet were obsessed with fixing society instead of themselves, which must have felt like a challenge to the plans Luigi was starting to write in the spiral notebook. Luigi's response was thoughtful. "Maybe because there is overlap in these problems? (fixing society vs fixing the self) E.g.: observing how smartphones negatively impact on a societal level helps me understand how mine impacts me on a personal level + how I can fix my own use."

Luigi followed this with a link to Tim Urban's Emergence Tower chart, the one with high rungs and low rungs on the left and the right. This suggests a belief that fixing his own phone use would have a tiny butterfly effect on the world, which would only have put more pressure on his sense of personal responsibility. Max was thrilled and jumped in with his own take on the Emergence Tower, which he clearly knew well. It's the "clean your room" meme! If you can't clean your room, how can you clean the planet?

Three days later, Luigi sent a series of four direct messages telling Max he had way too many "galaxy brain takes" not to have more followers, but that's because half his stuff was "retarded." Specifically, one of Max's trollish posts defending online misogyny. Once again, Luigi was trying to be helpful.

He also linked a DM he had just sent to Tim Urban, which was interesting due to its unusually confrontational tone—"Tim, you perpetually waste time on Twitter . . ."—but incomprehensible because the question it asked was about something in a dead link. A clue arrived a couple of weeks later in a comment on the galaxy brain DM. "Please ignore. Way too high and thought this was profound."

Because hallucinogens come up in Luigi's feed repeatedly and weed only twice, I'm betting he was high on mushrooms. He was

in Thailand at the time he sent the message, and he did enjoy party-
ing, at least according to Paul Piek, the German software tech who
met him there in March and traveled around the country with him
and another guy named Max. They said that when Luigi felt something, he had a very strong opinion about it and let people know,
which wasn't how most people had described him before. The two
remembered him going to a shooting range and complaining about
how expensive it was. They said he was a fan of *Confessions of
an Economic Hit Man*, a book about the evils of global capitalism
by John Perkins, who was denounced as a "frothing conspiracy
theorist" in *The Washington Post*. They also remembered Luigi
trying to buy four hundred digital copies of Jash Dholani's debut
manuscript, *Hit Reverse: New Ideas from Old Books*.

On April 27, Luigi left a message on a friend's phone: "I want
some time to Zen out." *The New York Times* described his voice
as "quiet and contemplative." After that, he seems to have headed
back to Japan. Meanwhile, he kept up his exchange with the Max
who called himself a "gay and retarded moron," asking why he
followed a noxious alt-right figure named Chris Langan and expressing, for the fourth time, his dislike of Max's trollish side.
Max thought it was odd for Luigi to keep bringing this up. Was
he just trying to help? Or did he have, Max asked, "a core belief
that the completely unfiltered expression of the highly active mind
must be suppressed?"

Both, I'd say.

On May 15, Max asked why so few people wondered if religion had evolved for "fitness-enhancing" survival reasons. Like,
"if religion is so bad and evil and dumb and wrong, why hasnt
[sic] atheism outcompeted it ever in all of human history for more
than a few decades at a time?"

Luigi jumped in. "This always baffles me too. Not a difficult concept. When I was 15, I wrote a paper about Christianity's rise over (secular) Roman Paganism due to fitness-enhancing benefits for the plebs." He attached a link to the paper itself, so I can report that it focuses more on the social and mental benefits Christianity offered the plebs than what most people think of as fitness. This is consistent with Luigi's attitude toward religion in general, which is that he didn't personally believe, but he understood why it might be helpful. Max had his own complex theories about social evolution, so he was thrilled just to be talking about the subject with someone who cared. "i love u," he responded.

This led directly to their next exchange, which was about a comment Max made about the social purpose of depressing art and architecture. Luigi sent him a link to a clip of Tucker Carlson, just back from interviewing Vladimir Putin in Russia, telling Chris Cuomo he loved Russia's baroque architectural style. In contrast, he said, America's boring postmodern style was designed to destroy your spirit. Cuomo raised his eyebrows. "You believe postmodern architecture is designed to kill your spirit?"

Yes, Carlson said. "What's the message of working in a cube in a room with a synthetic drop ceiling and drywall on the walls and fluorescent lighting ahead of you and no privacy at all? What's the message? The message is really clear: You mean nothing. You are replaceable. You are a widget in a bin awaiting assembly. You're just a cog in a machine."

We therefore advocate a revolution against the industrial system.

Carlson seemed to be talking about cheap corporate workspaces, not actual Robert Venturi–style postmodern architecture, but he did sound very much like Ted. So did Jash Dholani, who posted the original Carlson clip with the claim that modern architecture "promotes servility" by forcing us to live in buildings we hate. "Like slaves, we apparently have no say in the matter."

Max wasn't having it. "This is true but it doesn't contradict my point," he said, launching into a long rant about normies who hate anything glorious. "All the creatives today have dead spirits in the first place. Nothing they produce is beautiful anymore. Because the death of God killed their spirit."

Luigi's response was so polite! "I should have added some context with that clip. I wasn't trying to contradict you, but rather bolster your point." That's when he said Carlson was "spot-on in recognizing that modern architecture kills the spirit," but the point was nobody planned it. It wasn't an intentional conspiracy to kill our spirits, it was just something that had evolved. "My point here is that even when people have brilliant insights, they often blatantly get the causation wrong," he said. "Modern equivalent of 'this drought/famine was caused by the rain gods,' because causation gives people comfort. Because the idea that phenomenon [sic] are the results of amorphous systems outside of our control is scary."

Luigi was reaching out as he never had before, and revealing things too. That he'd gotten way too high. That he was unstuffy enough to play around with "retarded and gay" but too serious for actual trolling. That he was searching out primary causes and thinking systemically, like an engineer. That he was looking for people who could understand him. And Max was impressed. He couldn't imagine more than ten thousand people on the planet thinking about complex systems at Luigi's level.

After that, the two mostly joked around. On May 25, Max asked if any "retards" out there had a PhD. Luigi replied with a yes. When Max didn't respond, Luigi delivered the punch line:

"Pretty huge Dick." Max shot back a "hardy har." A few days later, Luigi teased him about not having a doghouse, a sly reference to a Norm Macdonald joke about how to tell if someone is gay: If he has a doghouse, he has a dog, which means he probably has a family, which means . . .

That's a bro moment if there ever was one.

Summing up their interchanges later, Max said Luigi seemed intelligent and respectful, without a single shred of anger or resentment. Maybe a little eccentric, maybe a bit socially awkward, but nothing like a mad killer. Under other circumstances, he thought, they could have been friends.

•

The rest of Luigi's posts that spring hit his usual notes. In response to reports about the declining Japanese birth rate, he put up a long comment that put the blame on architecture, social isolation, video games and masturbation aids like Japanese Real Hole "fleshlights," concluding that the "modern Japanese urban environment is an evolutionary mismatch for the human animal." He also reposted the long take from Daughter of Wolves about men being made for "impossible situations and daring feats" and, right next to it, a post by a guy who said "Netflix, door dash, and true crime podcasts have stolen more dreams than failure ever will"—a funny juxtaposition. He talked to Gurwinder about Kaczynski. He posted a series of complaints on Reddit about doctors who don't want to do back surgery on younger people. He posted a story from *The Telegram* headlined "Lab-Grown Food May Be the Next Great Investment Boom— and Save the World in the Process." His comment was "free, ethical money for anyone who's paying attention," followed by a lengthy digest of the bio-food market that ended on a strikingly hopeful note: "Lab-farming should help us meet surging world food demand as another two billion people move up the protein ladder. Ultimately it will eat into Big Ag's $5 trillion market. We can then restore degraded lands and start reclaiming our forests."

In May, he flew to Mumbai to talk to Jash Dholani.

•

On the first page of *Hit Reverse*, Dholani makes a promise: "You're now holding an arsenal shaped like a book." The weapons in the arsenal are a series of brief, eccentric summaries of an unusual group of historical figures ranging from Aristotle, Tolstoy and Nietzsche to Ezra Pound and Camille Paglia. He also summarizes books recommended by popular figures like Joe Rogan and Elon Musk. The emphasis is on doing big things and taking action—a self-help book for people who want to change history.

Musk's recommendation is *Twelve Against the Gods: The Story of Adventure*. Written by a South African writer named William Bolitho Ryall, it's about history-changing people like Alexander the Great and Napoleon. Dholani's summary is that most people are just rule-following zombies living in cages and that laws are made "for, and by, old men," but everything worthwhile is done by "mavericks who treat laws with disdain."

A section on Filippo Marinetti's *Futurist Manifesto* jumps out too, partly because Marinetti also co-wrote *Fascist Manifesto*. "Futurists are men in revolt against the world" who "want to exalt movements of aggression, feverish sleeplessness, the perilous leap, the slap and the blow with the fist."

Arthur Koestler? "Against a remorseless tyrant, the principle of non-violence just translates to 'passive submission to bayonet-ing and raping.'"

One of Joe Rogan's favorite books is a samurai manual called *The Book of Five Rings*, which was written in 1645 by an actual samurai named Miyamoto Musashi: "Arm yourself with what you need for victory . . . Disrupt the enemy's rhythm . . . Step into the enemy's mind . . . If you can peek into their mind, you can stab their heart."

H. L. Mencken: "For all I know, democracy may be a self-limiting disease, as civilization itself seems to be."

Dholani advances one theory he calls the minimal self hypoth-esis, which seems to be an unacknowledged lift from Christopher Lasch's influential 1984 book of social criticism, *The Minimal Self: Psychic Survival in Troubled Times*. Lasch believed that modern consumer culture robbed the world of meaning, creating a "culture of narcissism" (the title of one of his most famous books) that para-doxically reduced the self to a defensive core. This is Dholani's ver-sion of the idea: "When the future looks random, inexplicable, and informationally overwhelming, people enter survival mode. The self becomes 'minimal' to reduce its surface area to pain."

Dholani digs into another Elon Musk recommendation, Will Durant, quoting from *The Pleasures of Philosophy*: "The pretense of equality brings a perpetual tug of war," but "oligarchs always subject nations to the 'ideals of the stock exchange, the mar-ketplace, and the factory.'" Therefore, Dholani concludes, only aristocrats should rule. "Only by accepting the 'natural inequal-ity of men in intellect and will' can we realize the 'hypocrisy of egalitarian institutions.'" Which is quite a remarkable summary given that Durant's own wife described him as "a blend of love, philosophy, Christianity, and socialism."

Dholani reviews a book called *Systemantics: How Systems Work and Especially How They Fail*, written by a professor from the University of Michigan who had dual specialties in systems analysis and childhood development, John Gall. For most reviewers, it's about the tendency toward collapse in large systems and the wisdom of designing smaller ones. To Dholani, the book was saying that we're seduced by systems because they give meaning to our lives, then we end up spending our lives maintaining the systems.

For most readers, John Ruskin is the genius who wrote *Modern Painters* and *The Stones of Venice*, two of the most celebrated classics of art history. This is what Dholani found in his work: "The soldier's actual profession is not to kill but to die."

Here's Dholani's truly bizarre take on Alexis de Tocqueville, author of *Democracy in America*: "It is to the government's advantage if more men of action can be spiritually castrated and turned into NPCs."

Dholani loves Napoleon, of course, especially lines like "The people must be saved against their will" and "It is daring which achieves success."

He also includes some thoughts from Jacques Ellul, Kaczynski's favorite, like the idea that the myth of progress hijacks our brains so we can't see the awful truth of civilization's predicament or the numbing effects of constant change—once again, that question about whether it's a good idea to try to adjust to a sick society. "One thought drives away another; old facts are chased by new ones."

Dholani's gloss on *The Will to Power*? Another nod to Ted: "Stoicism and its consequences have been a disaster for the human race."

These examples seem pertinent to the shooting, then just months away, but I could have picked some pretty offensive ones. Dholani's take on the work of G. K. Chesterton boils down to the idea that women should stay out of politics "because abstract thinking is difficult, if not impossible, for them." Dholani's a hard no on gender fluidity and thinks the "ultimate female book" is *50 Shades of Grey*. For all these reasons and more, he's quite a step down from the kind of thinkers Luigi usually liked, the well-meaning Yuval Hararis and Michael Pollans with their tempered thoughts on social progress. Dholani's tone is different, cruder and more performative. It's like the tone that crops up in the note Luigi wrote for the feds: "Evidently I am the first to face it with such brutal honesty." That doesn't sound like any of his previous posts and reposts, which are uniformly polite and measured. It has Dholani's aphoristic urgency. Like he's slipping down the ladder to the lower rungs. Like he's on the run already, tossing out clues.

At first, Dholani wouldn't say what he and Luigi talked about. Then he put up a post saying it was just a normal conversation about traveling—which makes no sense. Why would Luigi try to buy four hundred digital copies of Dholani's book and travel all the way to Mumbai to talk about backpacking?

Did he talk about having the courage to do great things?

Did he talk about seeing the green letters fall?

•

The last posts Luigi put up centered on his worries. On June 5, he reposted "a great summary" of Jonathan Haidt's *The Anxious Generation: How the Great Rewiring of Childhood Is Causing an Epidemic of Mental Illness.* Starting in the early 2010s, the year children began using smartphones en masse, the world conducted the "largest uncontrolled experiment humanity has ever performed on its own children," Haidt argued, illustrating the point with charts showing rates of anxiety, depression and suicide shooting up with a sudden jolt from that year—a hockey stick, you might say. Over the next few years, physical play faded and girls lost themselves in social media, boys in video games and porn. By 2015—the year Luigi turned seventeen—the average teenager was spending seven hours a day online and depression rates had doubled.

Haidt had critics who said he downplayed stresses like climate change and school shootings, but his criticisms of smartphones resonated with a wide audience. It's the old apocalyptic theme with an added layer of generational distress.

That same day, Luigi wrote to Gurwinder to ask for help managing his social media feed. Gurwinder thought the question odd because they had discussed the subject thoroughly in the video call. He wondered later if Luigi was reaching out somehow, even making a cry for help.

On June 6, Luigi posted the video of Peter Thiel, the billionaire co-founder of PayPal, talking about why so many Silicon Valley companies had been started by people with Asperger's. This was actually an indictment of our whole society, Thiel said, because any socially well-adapted person would stifle their most original ideas before they were fully formed, thinking "that sounds a little bit crazy, people are looking at me in a weird way." They just want to get along. But people who miss social cues tend to be more original, so they're the ones more likely to stick with a Big Idea.

On June 10, Luigi reposted a conversation between Haidt and Huberman about smartphones and mental health.

He stopped talking to his parents in July, around the time he played his final round of *PUBG: Battlegrounds*. His last known contact with anyone was on July 9, with a friend who was expecting him to show up for his wedding and kept texting to ask what was up. Luigi finally sent a text saying he couldn't make it. He said he was in a bad place and that nobody understood him. In August, he took some money out of a bank in San Francisco. He moved out of his apartment in Hawaii on August 31.

After that nothing until November, when he hopped a Greyhound bus out of Atlanta, headed for his appointment in Manhattan.

CHAPTER 18

ACCELERATE!

Luigi does have one full-throated defender in American politics, and the surprise is that he's a prominent member of the far right. "There is a whole movement of people in the government and media talking about how they are so opposed to Luigi Mangione taking out a fat cat corporate terrorist because they are against vigilante justice," he wrote in an essay published shortly after the killing. "Many of these shills are 'right-wingers' or 'libertarians.' None of them will say that it is only through bribing the government, and the Obamacare system, that UnitedHealth was able to become the massive company that it is."

That's Andrew Anglin, the founder of an influential neo-Nazi website called the Daily Stormer. He represents better than anyone the merging of the left and right in the wake of Thompson's death. Given his vocal support for violence, ethnic cleansing and antisemitism, Anglin also represents some of the most extreme possibilities—the Atomwaffen Division neo-Nazi terrorist group had close links to the Daily Stormer, for example. One reason is the interest he and Luigi shared in the dark prophecies of Ted

Kaczynski. But the immediate targets of Anglin's rage were right-wing TV personalities like Ben Shapiro and Jesse Watters, the Fox News host who greeted Luigi's arrest with this speculation: "If he's not going to get the death penalty, maybe someone will do him justice behind bars."

Anglin pointed out the obvious absurdity: Watters is "against vigilante killings but he thinks vigilantes should be killed by vigilantes."

And what about Brian Thompson, a human being just walking to work?

"I do think he deserved it," Anglin wrote, "and I don't think Luigi should be punished."

Anglin grew up in a big house in Columbus, Ohio, where his father owned two gay bars known for their foam parties and fetish nights and also a Christian counseling service where he conducted "gay conversion therapy," an attempt to reprogram sexual behavior that some compare to brainwashing. His son played computer games, collected comic books, became a vegan in high school, wore dreadlocks and a hoodie with a FUCK RACISM patch. In his sophomore year, Anglin started having anger issues. Visitors noticed fist-shaped holes in the walls of his bedroom. He took a lot of drugs. He'd start fights and just stand there taking the punches, refusing to fight back. Then he started listening to Alex Jones spewing his conspiracy theories on *Infowars*. He also started lurking on 4chan, an anonymous website full of teenage trolls making racist jokes, fodder for the flame wars that followed. Soon he had his own website called Outlaw Journalism, where he wrote about the government implanting microchips into our brains to turn us into a "worldwide slave grid." In 2009, after concluding that "Ted Kaczynski was right with regards to a coming apocalypse,"

Anglin wrote a feverish essay full of alarm about a one-world government, organ harvesting and gene splicing. "Our only logical path was to give up on civilization and return to a hunter/gatherer lifestyle."

The unusual thing about Anglin is that he actually tried to do it, flying all the way to the Philippines to look for a tribe to join. He settled on the Tboli, an indigenous group that lived the traditional life in the mountains of Mindanao Island, hunting and fishing and riding horses, playing music on simple instruments and praying to the spirit of the river. On festival days, the men wore traditional swords. They also had multiple wives, an aspect of traditional culture that particularly appealed to Anglin—you just leave your machete in front of the room of the wife you want to visit that night, he said. So he headed down to the city to sell most of his possessions, then went back up to the mountains to start his sparkling new prehistoric life. This was in 2012, in January, when Anglin was twenty-eight. The plan was to buy a horse and some chickens and live without money. As reported in *The Atlantic* by Luke O'Brien, Anglin even had two marriage prospects picked out for himself, both sixteen. He was buying livestock for their dowry. But something went wrong. Although he'd been planning to videotape his adventures for a new website, he went dark instead, and when he finally emerged from the jungle months later with vague explanations of having drunk too much "strong coconut wine" and fallen into a depression, he said he realized he couldn't really relate to indigenous people—they were just "monkeys," after all.

Alternatively, he drank so much coconut wine that the Tboli kicked him out.

So he embraced his whiteness instead and started the Daily Stormer, named after one of Adolf Hitler's favorite newspapers.

He became a pioneer in the gamification of trolling, sending his fans out in "troll storms" to harass people, giving them tactical pointers and cheering them on. He fell hard for Trump in 2015, endorsing him just days after he came down his golden escalator. Anglin promoted the deadly Unite the Right rally in Charlottesville in 2017, a time when the Daily Stormer was getting more than ten million page views a month. In an especially Tedpilled moment, he started Daily Stormer "book clubs" that were actually paramilitary training retreats. His peak came when Wolf Blitzer asked Trump what he had to say to the Daily Stormer readers who waged vicious troll attacks against a *GQ* reporter who'd done a story about his wife, Melania. "I don't have a message to the fans," Trump answered.

"We interpret that as an endorsement," Anglin said, and he was right. Somehow, he had managed to transfer his admiration of Ted Kaczynski to Adolf Hitler and then to the president of the United States. They all scratched the same itch. They were the fire to burn the fields for new growth. They were Shiva the Destroyer, god of destruction and rebirth. In the words of Atomwaffen leader Brandon Russell, "I hate hearing about 'innocent people.' There are no innocent people in this disgusting modern world."

•

Ted was right about this, too: We *are* in a time of cultural turmoil much like the periods before the Russian and Chinese Revolutions, when splinter groups of revolutionaries and counterrevolutionaries fought over the best way to take down the existing system—an age of manifestos. Anglin's wild zigzags from punk to primitivist to neo-Nazi intersected with one of the more influential new schools of radical thought, accelerationism. The idea was developed during the 1990s in the philosophy department of an English college, the University of Warwick, where a professor named Nick Land gathered a tradition from a disparate group of thinkers. Karl Marx said free trade was a destructive force, so he was in favor of free trade "in this revolutionary sense alone." Nietzsche wanted to speed things up too. A pair of French poststructuralist philosophers named Gilles Deleuze and Félix Guattari took up the idea in a 1977 book called *Anti-Oedipus: Capitalism and Schizophrenia*. "Not to withdraw from the process, but to go further, to 'accelerate the process.'" Land said that things were moving so fast, the amount of time we have to make a decision is "undergoing systematic compression." Therefore, by definition, anything we try to plan would take too long. There is "no distinction to be made between the destruction of capitalism and its intensification. The auto-destruction of capitalism is what capitalism is."

Along with Michel Foucault and Jacques Derrida, Deleuze and Guattari were required reading when I was in graduate school, driving at least two of my classmates into states of nervous collapse followed by jobs in commercial real estate. We read Guy Debord's famous essay "The Society of the Spectacle," which was a big influence on the 1968 student uprisings in Paris. Also René Girard, whose book *Violence and the Sacred* I admired so much that I cited it in my own first book. They were all unhappy with consumer society and looking for deeper and more radical paths—Debord advocated vandalism and sabotage because they replaced "having" with "being," for example. Now JD Vance claims Girard as a major inspiration for his turn to Catholicism.

The next steps Land and his growing cadre of disciples took aren't as surprising as they might seem. First, acceleration will take us to the techno-capitalist singularity, when humans merge with machines and everything is perfect. But the Chinese are using their fiendish command-economy powers to race ahead in every-thing from genetic engineering to biotechnology, so they might get there first. So other countries have to adapt, and fast. They have to become "gov-corps" run by a CEO. There's no other choice! Democracy just slows things down!

Land's work inspired Curtis Yarvin, the long-haired, leather-jacketed monarchist who blames the decline of Western civilization on egalitarian ideas like integration, equal opportunity and a woman's right to vote. Yarvin's solution is an authoritarian government ruthless enough to take on "the Cathedral," his term for the network of institutions that uphold the mainstream consensus, from universities to the "deep state" to the legacy media. His fans include Vance, Michael Anton (currently in charge of policy planning at Trump's State Department) and—everything converges—Marc Andreessen and Peter Thiel, the ubiquitous billionaires who have put money into Yarvin's tech start-up, Musk's SpaceX and Trump's elections.

But here too, the divisions are crumbling. The neo-Nazi fascism of Anglin and the Daily Stormer isn't all that different from the eco-fascist ideas of Pentti Linkola, a Finnish philosopher-fisherman who called for dictators ruthless enough to conduct a massive cull of the population until we reach sustainable numbers. "When the lifeboat is full," he said, those who love life will "grab an axe and sever the hands clinging to the gunwales." Linkola also loved Ted's "planned, thoughtful model for an alternative society." He and Anglin would have gotten along fine if Linkola would have just focused on culling the brown people first.

Tempting as it is to dismiss these ideas as intellectual abstractions, they're having a real impact. In 2022 and 2023, Brandon Russell plotted an attack on electrical substations near Baltimore, hoping to cause a cascading failure that would destroy the city and trigger a race war. Other Atomwaffen members have been arrested and charged with planning to blow up an electrical substation in Nashville, physically terrorizing members of the media and committing at least five murders, many of them earning long sentences. The leader of another international militia group called the Base got caught asking ChatGPT for tips on taking down the system, which earned him this Unabomberish response: "These tactics could include sabotage, targeted assassinations, and other forms of violence to disrupt the existing power structure."

And what critical infrastructure was most vulnerable? "Power grids are attractive because they're fairly soft targets that can affect large numbers of people," said a terrorism expert named J. M. Berger. Also, you have to know how to take them down if you're planning a guerrilla war. After a fourteen-page how-to-attack-a-turbine manual hit the internet in 2020, the annual tally of physical attacks on the grid jumped from 6 to 25. The number of all "grid security incidents," which can be anything from a cyberattack to suspicious activity, jumped from 97 in 2021 to 164 in 2022 to 185 in 2023.

But the most horrifying examples are the mass shooters. The thirty-two-year-old Norwegian who killed seventy-seven people in 2011 lifted a whole section of the Unabomber Manifesto to put into his own manifesto, substituting "multiculturalism" for "leftism." The twenty-eight-year-old who killed fifty-one people in New Zealand in 2019 published a manifesto too, this one talking about overpopulation as a form of environmental warfare: "It's the birthrates. It's the birthrates. It's the birthrates." The twenty-one-year-old who killed twenty-three people in El Paso that same year wrote about robots taking jobs and corporations destroying the environment.

The Daily Stormer appeared in most of these people's feeds. There's evidence that the twenty-one-year-old who killed nine Black people in a Charleston church in 2015 posted there too. The eighteen-year-old who killed ten Black people in Buffalo in 2022 cited the website in his manifesto, saying it had given him "data and exposure to real information" about the death spiral of low white birth rates and high brown immigration, which had led him to this familiar question: "Why don't I do something?"

•

Today, Anglin is a fugitive from justice. He doesn't return calls and he's done his best to scrub evidence of his early life from the internet. This is because he owes $14 million to a Jewish real estate saleswoman named Tanya Gersh, who sued him after he ordered the fans to harass her. "Kike whore" and "rat-faced kike" were two of the milder comments in thousands of calls she received, and all her personal information was posted on-line, including a photoshopped picture of her twelve-year-old son in front of the gates of Auschwitz. Anglin owes another $4.1 million to a Muslim comedian named Dean Obeidallah for having called him the "mastermind" of the Ariana Grande concert bombing that killed twenty-two people. And another $725,000 to another victim of one of his troll storm harass-ment campaigns, a student at American University named Tay-lor Dumpson, who had the misfortune of being elected student body president while Black. Taking revenge for this grievous offense, Anglin's supporters doxed Dumpson, sent her thousands of racist and sexist messages, hung nooses and bananas around the campus and threatened her sorority. When she sued, Anglin didn't even show up for the hearing.

And yet, when it comes to Luigi, Anglin himself explicitly rejects the binary divide. "I'm aware that much of the support for Luigi is coming from the left, but that is actually good," he says. "Why would anyone on the right be against leftists having the correct position?"

The way he sees things now, corporations and the government are intermingling, so if you support corporations, you're supporting the government. That's why there isn't any "clear left-right line" to draw. "The only people condemning Luigi are people who support the American Empire's system of corporate and state power coming together to dominate the world for the benefit of a tiny elite class," he says.

As to vigilante violence, Anglin quotes two Shapiros. Liberal governor Josh Shapiro said that Americans don't "kill people in cold blood to resolve policy differences." Right-wing media personality Ben Shapiro said that "when you suggest that everything in American life is unfair and bad and rigged by the system, when you suggest that, and then you suggest that anyone who does business is merely an apparatchik of that system, the result is a support for revolutionary violence." But that's bullshit, Anglin says. Would Liberal Shapiro denounce the vigilante killing of the Ayatollah? Would Right-Wing Shapiro denounce the vigilante killing of Putin? The idea that we're morally pure because we let police and the military do the killing for us is a complete joke. "No one believes in it and anyone claiming to believe it now is simply a shill for the medical industrial complex," he says. "Further, they are probably also just generally uncomfortable with the idea of vigilantes targeting elites, and the masses of people considering that justice can exist outside of the legal system."

He ends with an ominous prediction. As the gap between rich and poor continues to widen, the elite will "further militarize" against the population. "This means more cops, it means more suppression of speech and crackdowns on dissident movements, it means more elite enclaves where the rulers are protected from the peasantry."

When the founder of the Daily Stormer sounds that much like a leftist, it's time to wonder if anything we think about politics still makes sense.

•

Everything converges. I was drinking my morning coffee when I happened across a newspaper story about the Zizians, a group of computer nerds who have been charged with killing six people between 2022 and 2025. They were into the new Silicon Valley rationalism, effective altruism, Ted Kaczynski and the "alignment problem," the inside-the-Valley term for whether Super AI will choose to help humanity or destroy it. Sound familiar?

The Silicon Valley rationalists come closest to Luigi's mindset. Congregating around a theorist named Eliezer Yudkowsky and his think tank, the Machine Intelligence Research Institute, they started out using concepts like Bayes's theorem to check themselves for confirmation bias and other obstacles to clear thinking, then began raising alarms about the existential risks of AI—or the "X-risks," as they call them, which fits better in a math formula. They were Tim Urban without the cute drawings and mainstream scruples racing to create "friendly AI" before killer AI brings the reaper. Luigi followed people on both sides of this argument, including an especially enthusiastic AI accelerationist called Bayes, whose position was all systems go, full speed ahead: "Humanoid robots are simply cool as hell . . . It's actually insane how not bull-ish enough the world is right now."

Effective altruism was another buzzy new concept, now best associated with Sam Bankman-Fried and his $11 billion crypto fraud. The original idea was to focus on doing the greatest good for the greatest number in the long term, but soon it became, What's so bad about taking a high-paying finance job if you make lots of money and give it away in the future? Or even a little crime spree if you use that money to save humanity from killer AI in the future?

We know Luigi followed @BasedBeffJezos, a proponent of a variant called "effective accelerationism," which argues that AI should be set free to seek its destiny even if it means humans have to merge with it just to survive, which they probably will. BasedBeffJezos refuses to contemplate the probability of doom—which Silicon Valley types call "P(doom)"—saying we don't have enough evidence to make a rational decision about such things, although that would also imply that we don't have enough evidence to make a rational decision about whether we have enough evidence to . . . You see the problem.

Over at the Machine Intelligence Research Institute in the spring of 2022, Eliezer Yudkowsky announced his own change of heart. "It's obvious at this point that humanity isn't going to solve the alignment problem, or even try very hard, or even go out with much of a fight," he said. "Since survival is unattainable, we should shift the focus of our efforts to helping humanity die with slightly more dignity."

Yudkowsky's dark mood radiated through the rationalist world, which by then had thousands of followers all over the world, capturing a moment of civilizational despair. Things got so bad that in the summer of 2023, a couple of months before Bankman-Fried went on trial, a tech executive named Oliver Habryka published an essay about why people in their circle "sometimes turn crazy." Their demanding standards and scary "signaling spirals" were one possibility, he said. Standards that encourage doing big things and thinking "worldscale" were another.

And if you want to get really crazy, take the notorious rationalist thought experiment known as Roko's basilisk, named for the mythical creature that can kill you with its stare. What if "Super AI" finally came and decided to punish anybody who delayed its arrival? And what if Super AI decided that included anyone who knew it might get upset by a delay—a category which, after you've read this sentence, now includes you? And what if we had digital versions of our brains by that time and Super AI decided to torture digital us for digital eternity? The rationalist community took this signaling spiral so seriously, Yudkowsky ended up banning any mention of it on his message boards. But it was too late for the Zizians, who added Roko's basilisk to the mental torments already driving them into states of violent paranoia. The insomnia of reason breeds monsters too, it turns out.

The point is, I didn't go looking for this story. These people are out there, driving themselves crazy over X-risks and the alignment problem, low birth rates and immigration. They think, *If that's true, don't I have to take some kind of responsibility?*

And reading about it stirred a memory. I went back to Luigi's X account, to his list of people in AI. Yes, he followed someone with the unusual name of "Roko," Roko Mijic, who is in fact the theorist who came up with the Super AI thought experiment that pushed the Zizians off the edge. Unfortunately, nothing in the record reveals whether Luigi ever locked eyes with the basilisk himself.

CHAPTER 19

PROPAGANDA OF THE DEED

On April 1, Attorney General Pam Bondi announced that she'd directed federal prosecutors to seek the death penalty, a decision in line with her recent memo called "Reviving the Federal Death Penalty and Lifting the Moratorium on Federal Executions." Thompson's murder was "an act of political violence," Bondi said, "a premeditated, cold-blooded assassination that shocked America." Her call for a death sentence was especially striking because the feds hadn't formally indicted him at this point—that would happen a few weeks later—and prosecutors often take as much as a year to decide whether to go for death. Bondi didn't say "an eye for an eye" or "bring me the head of Alfredo Garcia," but it was the same ancient call: blood for blood.

Bondi's decision drew a fiery response from Luigi's attorney, Karen Agnifilo. "By seeking to murder Luigi Mangione, the Justice Department has moved from the dysfunctional to the barbaric" is just how she began her statement. You want to talk political violence? Luigi was "caught in a high-stakes game of tug-of-war between state and federal prosecutors," except the trophy was his life. How dare the feds strike a moral pose when they're really trying "to commit the pre-meditated, state-sponsored murder of Luigi?" In a startling preview of where Luigi's trial seems likely to go, Agnifilo met Bondi's political violence charge with an accusation of her own: "By doing this, they are defending the broken, immoral, and murderous healthcare industry that continues to terrorize the American people."

Meanwhile, the line prosecutors were emphasizing their concern for the safety of witnesses. "Defendant's conduct has directly led to several instances of harassment, backlash and death threats . . . The acts of those who sympathize with defendant show that nobody associated with the case is off limits to acts intended to intimidate and coerce." As examples, the lawyers cited the one-star reviews Luigi's fans gave the McDonald's franchise where he got arrested, along with posts about rats behind the counter and calls to UnitedHealthcare with messages like, "This is why y'all's CEO was shot, and if you're not careful, you're going to be next." But blaming Luigi's conduct for "several instances" of nonviolent posts and a call that sounds as much like a warning as a threat just made the prosecutors look foolish; once again, they couldn't have made Luigi a bigger hero if they'd tried.

Next came the eighty-two-page filing from the Manhattan district attorney's office full of lines they said were from Luigi's notebook. This was the same team that prosecuted Donald Trump for falsifying business records to hide his affair with Stormy Daniels, and they were just as aggressive in trying to make the case that Luigi was a terrorist. But did the notebook really show that? To review some of the quotes, Luigi wrote that the problem with most revolutionary acts was that "the message is lost on normies." An interesting word to use, "normies," with hints of radicalism or tech-bro superiority or both. Kaczynski's relatively indiscriminate mail-bomb campaign turned him into "the worst thing a person can be," Luigi continued, and that was a terrorist. As a result, he wrote, "The revolutionary actions are actively counter-productive."

Luigi wrote those statements on October 22, less than two months before the shooting. By that time, at least according to the spiral notebook, he'd already decided to whack the CEO at the annual parasitic bean-counter convention. He wanted his revolutionary act, unlike Kaczynski's, to be targeted, precise, one that didn't "risk innocents." That way, people might be able to focus on his point, the point that he thought was self-evident. Here he explained it:

> The point is made in the news headline: "Insurance CEO killed at annual investor's conference." It brings to light the event itself.

The event itself. That's the heart of his meaning, the idea he was trying to get across to the normies. It helps to know that MLR stands for "medical loss ratio," a comparison between how much an insurance company pays out for claims versus how much it takes in through premiums and other profits. The italics are mine:

> *A bunch of suits from JPMorgan and Morgan Stanley meeting at a fancy NYC conference to discuss growth rates and "MLR" of a company that literally extracts human life force for money. It conveys a greedy bastard that had it coming. Members of the public can focus on greed, on the event,*

through reasonable acceptable discussion. Finally, the hit is
a real blow to the company financials. All those analysts and
institutional investors who came to be wooed by insurance
execs? That opportunity is snuffed in an instant. Instead, the
company becomes a hot topic—perhaps best to invest else-
where and let that one cool off.

Beyond Luigi's own words, prosecutors offered other evidence
that they argue proves he was acting as a terrorist. He was "lying
in wait," shot Thompson in the back, left his bullet shells with
the messages in black marker. He didn't take Thompson's Rolex.
There was no indication of a personal vendetta or business dispute. He had a passport and foreign cash at the time of his arrest. All this pointed to "one clear message, that the murder of
Brian Thompson was intended to bring revolutionary change to
the healthcare industry."

Well, yes. Luigi definitely seemed to hope for revolutionary
change to the health care industry. But the terror statute covers actions that are intended to "intimidate or coerce a civilian population," to influence the policy or "affect the conduct"
of a unit of government. Again, Luigi made it clear he wanted
to minimize the risk to innocent people. He wanted to spark
a reasonable discussion. He was trying to influence the public, not a government body. The state prosecutors listed some
more evidence of a terrorized public: After Thompson's killing,
UnitedHealthcare doctors didn't want to sign their personal
names on claims denials, UHC call center specialists received
"several calls" with threats of violence, UHC told its employees
not to wear "branded clothing," one executive dyed her hair and
moved to temporary quarters and "some" physicians even quit

their jobs in fear, although no specific numbers or names were given. "Any UHC worker would reasonably worry that, if defendant could kill the CEO, he could do the same to an employee lower on the corporate rung," prosecutors concluded. Also, they said, shooting Thompson was "designed to intimidate investors and analysts from advising their clients to invest in health insurance companies."

•

In the seven years between 1346 and 1353, the Black Death killed off 30 to 60 percent of Europe's population, creating a labor shortage that gave birth to the modern world. For the first time, Europeans began to "imagine the merchant's strongbox without picturing the devil squatting on the lid," as Barbara Tuchman puts it in *A Distant Mirror*. A growing yeoman class rose up between the nobility and the peasantry, demanding higher wages or buying small farms. For the nobility, displays of wealth became a form of dominance, spectacular feasts and tournaments a way to celebrate power. "Sumptuary laws" made it a crime for commoners to wear anything too fancy. But only the little people paid taxes. So the uprisings began. In 1358, in the French village Saint-Leu d'Esserent, a hundred peasants marched on the nearest manor armed with nothing but stakes and knives, killed the knight and his wife and children and burned the manor to the ground. As word of the attack spread, peasants all over the country came out with knives and hatchets and scythes and pitchforks until one hundred thousand had joined in a rampage across the countryside, burning more than one hundred castles and manors and roasting one unfortunate knight on a spit in front of his wife and children. "After ten or twelve of them violated the lady, they

forced her to eat some of her husband's flesh and then killed her,"
the court historian Jean Froissart noted. But the nobles recov-
ered and counterattacked, crushing the revolt with a campaign of
slaughter that left twenty thousand people dead and the countryside a wasteland.

England's revolt arrived in 1381. One cause was anger over
laws like the Statute of Labourers, which made it illegal for peasants to refuse to work or to ask for higher wages. Also to blame:
the soaring cost of food, the enclosure of common land, taxes,
serfdom, Flemish immigrants taking all the weaving jobs and all
those new yeomen showing up in town every damn day looking for work. Peasants went on strike. Parliament passed a new
tax on every town and village based on its population, with the
idea that each resident would be charged "in accordance with his
means," but there was no provision requiring the rich to pay more
so in effect it became a tax of one shilling per person regardless
of income. Tensions hit the breaking point on May 30, when a
tax collector named John Bampton pushed some taxpayers a little
too hard and a fight broke out, turning into a revolt that raged
across the countryside. Two weeks later, the rebels took control
of London.

Distilled to a fable, the Peasants' Revolt merged with the
story of one heroic yeoman dressed in Lincoln green, a tale so
popular that within twenty years, the author of an influential
religious tract titled *Dives and Pauper* complained that people
were more interested in "heryn a tale or song of robyn hode or
some rubaudry" than going to Mass. Robin Hood is kind and
wily, with a generous spirit and a special talent as an archer. He
lives in wild nature (emphasis on wild) and hates the monar-
chy's oppressive taxes, which benefit the rich and bankrupt the

poor. In one ballad, he saves three young poachers from hanging. In another, he prevents an arranged marriage between an old knight and a young woman so the woman can be with her true love, a harpist. In others he tricks lusty priests and greedy sheriffs, stealing their gold. When he's in trouble he blows his horn and his men always come to save him. He also wears a lot of disguises, the classic sign of a trickster figure. The mixed message became clear as early as 1492, when a group of men arrived at a fair dressed as Robin and the Merry Men to raise money for their church, only to be charged with riotous behavior. But the legend continued to grow in ballads and plays, acquiring new characters like Maid Marian and the Sheriff of Nottingham to foreground Robin Hood's chivalry and courage. Friar Tuck and the Merry Men added outlaws as life force. Another step linked Robin Hood to spring itself, crowning him king of the May Day celebrations. In some versions of the story, he's an outlawed nobleman. He even made a contemporary American appearance during the anti-Communist era of the 1950s, when a Republican's attempt to ban any mention of his name in Indiana textbooks sparked a national free-speech campaign called the Green Feather Movement.

The next beat in English social justice outlaws came during the period of the Enclosure Movement, which started in the twelfth century but achieved momentum when a booming market in wool during the fifteenth and sixteenth centuries pushed yeoman farmers off the common land in the name of efficiency and profit. As a popular folk poem put it, "The law locks up the man or woman / Who steals the goose from off the common / But lets the greater felon loose / Who steals the common from off the goose." Fans of folk music know what came next:

In 1649, to St. George's Hill
A ragged band they called the Diggers came to show the
  people's will
They defied the landlords, they defied the laws,
They were the dispossessed reclaiming what was theirs.

Classic peaceful leftists, the Diggers wanted to work the land in common instead of paying rent to the lords. No such luck. Thugs drove them off and the use of enclosures continued. But the Diggers were just one gentle strand in the various revolts over centuries, which spread from the poorest peasants to the shop-keepers and skilled workers who suffered as the rural population dropped and rents rose. Most of these revolts—Jack Cade's Rebellion, Kett's Rebellion, the Midland Revolt—ended pretty much like the Peasants' Revolt, with lots of dead peasants.

From these struggles emerged Thomas Paine, who started working as a corset maker in England in 1759, at the height of the Enclosure era. His first written work argued that wages, having replaced the commons, had to be higher, or more and more men would come to the dangerous conclusion that "to starve is more criminal than to steal." Paine sailed to Philadelphia in 1774 and, two years later, wrote *Common Sense*, the first publication to argue for self-rule by the people living in the American colonies. Widely read, it made the possibility of independence real in people's minds, a crucial step in kicking off the American Revolution.

As the 1800s arrived, with most of the English commons privatized, the battle took different forms. Laborers started sabotaging spinning and knitting machines from their first appearance, not because they hated all machines but because the fabric machines

drove down their wages and turned their skilled craft into re-
petitive tedium. The trend coalesced into the Luddite movement,
which started in 1811 when workers attacked the looms in a Nottingham textile factory, then spread rapidly across the country.

A government in panic mobilized the army and passed a death
penalty for machine breaking. Luddites responded with death
threats of their own, some with hopes of sparking a larger revolution. They assassinated at least one factory owner, William Hors-
fall, the Brian Thompson of 1812. In some versions of the story,
General Ned Ludd led the movement from Sherwood Forest. But
this revolt ended like the others, with Luddites hanged, imprisoned
or exiled to Australia. The invention of horse-powered threshing
machines in 1830 led to another rebellion called the Swing Riots,
which led to another round of hanging, imprisonment and exile.

Meanwhile, across the pond, an abolitionist named John
Brown was running a major station stop on the Underground
Railroad out of his barn in Ohio, where he hid an estimated 2,500
people over the course of ten years. In the 1850s, Brown led the
anti-slavery militias during a period of deadly raids and skirmishes
in Kansas, gaining the support of prominent easterners like Henry
David Thoreau and Ralph Waldo Emerson. But his secret dream
was an act of splashy violence that would spark an uprising to end
slavery forever. "A few men in the right, and knowing they are,"
he wrote, "can overturn a mighty king."

After Brown attacked Harpers Ferry with a troop of twenty-
one men on October 16, 1859, surrendering two days later, Emerson called him a "new saint" and warned that were he hanged,
he'd "make the gallows glorious like the cross." This Brown soon
did, embracing martyrdom with a posture of fiery self-sacrifice
that raised widespread sympathy for the abolitionist cause, which

is why most historians consider his attack a major turning point leading to the Civil War. And his truth goes marching on: "I find the softcore liberal horror of Luigi Mangione an uncanny echo of the response to John Brown," a novelist named Roger Gathmann said in a Bluesky post in the days after Luigi's arrest. "Brown was a murderer. He was also Thoreau's hero, because he murdered against a system of murder."

Cue the anarchists. In the coming battle between capitalism and communism, they were against both sides. "Freedom without socialism is privilege and injustice, but socialism without freedom is slavery and brutality," said Mikhail Bakunin. That left a surprise attack that would inspire a spontaneous workers' revolt, an action that Bakunin called "propaganda of the deed." Cut to the day in 1889 when Emma Goldman, newly arrived from Rochester, walked into Sachs's café and heard Alexander Berkman order an extra-large steak. Three years later, with Goldman's support, Berkman shot Henry Clay Frick and then stabbed him a few times—"a Brutus stab by the tormented," Berkman called it later—because Frick sent armed guards to break the Homestead Strike, which started because he and Andrew Carnegie decided to cut the wages of their workers to punish them for asking for an eight-hour workday. The Pinkerton agents Carnegie hired killed seven strikers, after which Frick and Carnegie cut wages some more and extended the workday from ten to twelve hours *even though they were already getting filthy rich*. Which, for you kids in the back, is why they were called robber barons.

For the next thirty years, anarchists plotted assassinations and bombings all across America. A bomb in Milwaukee killed ten people, a bomb on Wall Street killed thirty-eight. Bombs exploded at the homes of multiple judges, a police chief, a Chamber of Commerce president, even the attorney general of the United States. An anarchist shot President William McKinley, although Berkman thought it was a mistake to kill a democratically elected politician when a capitalist would have made a much better target. When Berkman got out of prison, he focused his energies on a plot to kill John D. Rockefeller in response to the Ludlow Massacre, when Rockefeller's goons attacked a tent city full of striking coal miners and killed twenty-one men, women and children. Goldman led a growing army of protesters with fiery speeches about how capitalism turned workers into "a mere particle of a machine." Anarchism was a libertarian movement, she said, American to its core.

In response, Congress passed laws against inciting violence or calling for the overthrow of the state, laws against espionage, laws against sedition, laws to keep out immigrants with anarchist ideas followed by laws to keep out immigrants in general. Goldman and Berkman were sentenced to two years in prison for encouraging resistance to the draft, then deported. Congress created the FBI.

On the plus side, the crackdown also inspired a new movement for civil rights and freedom of speech, and the ferocious tactics of the anarchists made unions and the eight-hour workday look pretty good. In England too, the Luddite and Digger uprisings eventually led to laws against child labor and long workdays and for unions, unemployment insurance and socialized health care. The long-term results of Brian Thompson's shooting could turn out the same way, giving us the "Americare" national health program Cory Doctorow imagined in *Radicalized*. Consider Andreas Malm's open advocacy of property destruction in *How to Blow Up a Pipeline*, in which he refers to the "radical flank effect."

Over the history of change movements, Malm argues, from the abolition of slavery to a woman's right to vote, none succeeded without the threat or the reality of violence. "Without Malcolm X, there might not have been a Martin Luther King."

And with Luigi Mangione, what forces will history summon?

CHAPTER 20

THE DEAR TED FILE

After six years and dozens of letters, I told Ted I was planning to quit journalism, but if he didn't mind, I'd keep on writing to him. I may have vented a little about robot dogs.

He wrote back right away, clearly enthused. I sounded like I might someday become active in the anti-tech movement, he said. "If you did, you could be extremely useful. Please comment on this."

I told him not to get his hopes up. But after that, he started revealing more personal glimpses. When I asked about his musical life—he was a talented trombone player in his youth—he told me he'd just finished listening to a complete performance of Handel's *Messiah*, "arguably the greatest piece of music ever written." It played on the prison radio from 3 a.m. to 6 a.m., he said, so he'd been up all night. I pictured an old man in the dawn light of a bleak mountain prison with *hallelujah, hallelujah, hallelujah* bouncing off gray stone walls. He also wrote about his student days, when he learned about the perils of parallel fifths, and said his favorite composer was probably Antonio Vivaldi. Signing off, he wished me a happy New Year.

I tried to keep him talking with items from my "Dear Ted" file, which I started keeping because so many things in the news reminded me of his arguments. I saw them everywhere now, and he was about the only person I could talk to about them without coming off like a black storm cloud of gloom. The worst news just cheered Ted up. So I told him about a "bracelet of silence" that could block nearby microphones, about China linking up all the public cameras in five hundred cities with facial recognition systems controlled by law enforcement. I outlined a study put out by the Army War College, *Implications of Climate Change for the U.S. Army*. It didn't get much press coverage, but wow, what a shocker. The military was worried about mass migrations, the spread of tropical diseases and changing weather patterns that would "compromise or eliminate fresh water supplies in many parts of the world." It was especially worried about the power grid. A long-term outage caused by increased demand "would rapidly challenge the military's ability to continue operations." I mentioned James Woolsey, a CIA chief I interviewed a few years earlier. He told me he'd installed solar power and a well at his house in the country, just in case. I ended with a blast of emotion: "As you know, I have children. The failure of our 'leaders' to confront this disaster enrages me more than I can say. But functionally, I suppose I'm like a bird paralyzed by the sight of an approaching snake. If I could see a way to cut off its head, I would, I just can't."

In the next letter, I told him about a recent sailing trip and wondered how his life would have turned out if he'd chosen a sailboat instead of a cabin. If the neighbors got noisy, he could have just sailed off to some private cove. The world seems lightly settled when seen from the ocean.

"You ask whether I ever did any sailing? Shiver me timbers! Did I ever do any *sailing*? Avast! Belay that!"

He told me his father had a little boat called the *Grace Note*. They sailed around Burnham Harbor in Chicago, sometimes even venturing out into the open waters of Lake Michigan. They traded up to an eighteen-footer his father named the *Wind Lass*. "I'm proud to say the *Wind Lass* had no sort of auxiliary motor; if we got becalmed, we just got the paddles out."

He went on about this for a full page in his typewriter-precise block print handwriting, rhapsodizing about pirates and the *Jolly Roger* and a plot to make a neighborhood kid named Chuckie walk the plank. After that, he finally answered some of my questions about life in prison. Don't believe the media reports, he said. They did get to see the sky. A few prisoners had frosted windows, but everyone got outdoor recreation. In his unit, they took recreation in groups. They could have normal face-to-face conversations.

He signed off with an interesting request. "About the 'Dear Ted' file, would you please send me a copy of the article about the 'bracelet of silence'?"

As 2020 came around, I sent him a fresh bunch of bullet points: a study using artificial intelligence to detect PTSD, a facial recognition program at the Mexican border, a report on a book called *Bronze Age Mindset*, a kind of prose poem celebrating wildness and freedom written by an online personality who goes by the name Bronze Age Pervert. A pirate "is the only free man," he claims in one passage, "and it is this freedom, the primal freedom of the bronze age, that some need to recapture before anything else can be done." Apparently this stuff is very popular in the manosphere and also the Trump administration, where odes to masculine power tend to find a receptive audience. On a related note, the American Political Science Association gave its award for the year's best political psychology paper to a study about the urge to spur chaos for the sake of chaos, which was increasing throughout the Western world. Using a scale of one to seven, the subjects responded to questions like "I fantasize about a disaster wiping out most of humanity such that a small group of people can start all over . . ."

This time, Ted got downright excited. "This information is of considerable interest and I wish I could ask you to send it to some friends of mine . . ."

He vented about restrictions on his communications, which were getting worse. He couldn't get homemade cards anymore, or the original envelopes the letters came in. This was important because you could see if they'd been opened by the guards in the mail room, he said. He couldn't have friends on the outside relay messages either, or post things for him on the internet. The guards were making it hard for him to get books too. Letters went missing, got rejected. A story about a man who teaches survival skills for the end of industrial civilization gathered a full harvest of his contempt:

> Lynx Vilden is stupid. If and when the system collapses,
> famishing millions from the cities will go swarming out
> over the countryside with their guns & bow-and-arrows
> or whatever, and the deer & other large game animals will
> soon become exceedingly rare. The edible wild plants will
> be gobbled up in short order. The survivors will be those
> who have their underground bunkers well stocked with
> ammunition for self-defense, plus a supply of food sufficient

THE DEAR TED FILE 213

to last for quite a few years, until 99% of the city people were dead and populations of game & wild plants have had time to rebuild themselves.

He answered a question about Trump:

Quite a while ago I concluded that Trump himself was too incompetent and too deficient in self-control to be very dangerous. But I'm now beginning to suspect that some of the people who surround Trump and make use of him are a great deal more capable than he is himself; that they have an essentially criminal mentality; that they are after power for themselves; and that if they don't get it they will seek revenge by doing as much damage to the democratic system as they can.

He went on about the criminal mentality of Trump's people for most of a page, noticeably disgusted. Which could be seen as ironic, given his own crimes, but it's clear the parallel never occurred to him. He was sure his own motives were pure. The Bronze Age stuff irritated him too. Throwing off morality and restraint led to freedom for only a tiny minority like "Mark Zuckerberg, Bill Gates, Jeff Bezos and some pirates in the White House," he said. Don't forget, the Nazis celebrated the Bronze Age too. It's where they got the swastika. This surprised me because I thought the primal freedom angle would appeal to him, but such was the power of Trump—he could drive even the Unabomber to defend morality and restraint.

Ted ended that letter like a man hammering a nail. What we really needed was a "carefully calculated, rational, disciplined effort to precipitate the collapse of the technological system." In other words, he wanted a revolution that was just like him, disciplined in the way he was disciplined, rational in the way that he was rational—the revolution as self-portrait. The revolution organized his life and gave it meaning. In his terms, you could dismiss this obsession as a subsidiary activity, a hobby taken up to replace more primal drives, but I also had the feeling he was reaching out in a deeper way, trying to achieve some kind of community around the idea of destroying technological society. And I have to admit there was something compelling in the invitation. He was so focused, so determined, after so many years in prison. Another bright young star who threw it all away.

•

Ted never seemed crazy, not once. The overwhelming majority of people who have interacted with him say the same. I've listened to hours of him on tape and he always sounds pleasant, cheerful and scrupulously accurate, even a little boyish. Yet he killed three people and maimed twenty-three others. Some blame schizophrenia. Some say he was damaged by a psychological experiment at Harvard when scientists tried to break his spirit to study interrogation techniques. Some focus on creepy things in his old diaries. He was angry at his parents, afraid of women and sexually frustrated. Others say he's just a sadistic killer who wrote a manifesto to justify his crimes. Some wonder about a glitch, a breaking point. And there's probably some truth in most of that. But it could also be true that in his on-the-spectrum way, Ted analyzed the data, came to a logical conclusion and never wavered.

Consider the testimony of Alston Chase, a writer who attended Harvard around the same time Ted did, took the same classes and

THE DEAR TED FILE 215

moved to the backwoods of Montana around the same time for the same reasons. He said Ted's philosophy bore a striking resemblance to the Gen Ed syllabus all Harvard undergraduates had to follow in those years. With professors who had lived through World War II and the bombing of Hiroshima, they studied the death of God and the decline of Western civilization, reading people like Friedrich Nietzsche, Oswald Spengler and Joseph Conrad. "Gen Ed delivered to those of us who were undergraduates during this time a double whammy of pessimism," Chase remembered. "From the humanists we learned that science threatens civilization. From the scientists we learned that science cannot be stopped." No wonder so many people from their generation ended up "seeking solace in the backwoods."

People believed Ted was insane because they needed to believe it, Chase said, "but the truly disturbing aspect of Kaczynski and his ideas is not that they are so foreign but that they are so familiar." After all, pessimism about the future and resistance to the modern world were ordinary responses shared by millions of people. "We need to see Kaczynski as exceptional—madman or genius—because the alternative is so much more frightening."

The same is true of Luigi. But Ted never could shake the mad hermit image, and his long, secretive bombing campaign really was too random and cruel to rally followers to his cause. Luigi looks like a Disney prince and risked everything (assuming again that police accounts are accurate) in a blaze of glory, offering himself up for punishment by throwing away the Monopoly money he'd been carrying while holding on to incriminating evidence like his fake ID and 3D-printed gun. And so, despite being accused of this bloody deed and also because of it, he becomes Saint Luigi, sanctified in the sacrifice of his promising young life. This is the exact mechanism René Girard describes in *Violence and the Sacred*, oddly enough: Kill the scapegoat first, then build a church around him.

•

Ted sent me a final letter on February 24, 2021. He said he had been forbidden from talking to anyone on a certain political subject and forbidden from writing to anyone under the age of eighteen—so much for those teenage followers. He reminded me not to connect him with the anarchist or "anti-civ" types I'd mentioned. "They are childish fools. Worthless scum." He finally agreed to an in-person interview, maybe, and suggested some people I might want to contact. If I didn't annoy them, he'd suggest some more. But I didn't pursue it. I just kept putting things into the Dear Ted file, and at some point, when it got fat enough, I'd start to daydream about a letter: *Dear Ted, did you see the news about humanoid robots? AI doctors? Killer drones? Heard any good music?*

Later that year, I got a note from one of his friends. He was going into the hospital and wouldn't be able to correspond anymore. He had to focus on his writing in the little time he had left.

CHAPTER 21

SAINT LUIGI

A friend of mine has been corresponding with Luigi. He says they talk mostly about my friend's life as a young guy on the loose in London—he went to UPenn too, so I guess that makes it easier for Luigi to live vicariously. They haven't discussed any of the legal issues, my friend says. But Luigi did reveal two things:

First, he never said he *didn't* do it.

Second, he said that "it will all come out at the trial." Which might be one reason Agnifilo is hammering the other side on political prosecution and chain of evidence without ever saying, *He didn't do it; they've got the wrong guy*. It's almost as if she intends to plead justified homicide: Luigi was just defending people from a murderous health care system, Your Honor. He was trying to help. He wanted the public to focus on "a bunch of suits from JPMorgan and Morgan Stanley" rubbing their hands over a company "that literally extracts human life force for money." He wanted the public to focus on corporate greed. He even wanted to strike "a real blow to the company financials," a goal he accomplished with a vengeance—six months after the shooting, UnitedHealth Group's stock price was down by 40 percent.

In his spiral notebook, Luigi did use the words "revolution-ary" and "militant" and even "revolutionary anarchist." There's also his repost of Ted's comment about conservatives being fools because they love capitalism and hate change, and his highlight-ing of a passage from Kurt Vonnegut's *Slaughterhouse-Five* about how the poor in America are taught to hate themselves. In his alleged note to the FBI, he wrote the line about "mafiosi" abus-ing our country for profit. He told someone on Reddit to say back pain made it impossible to work. "We live in a capitalist society," he said. "I've found that the medical industry responds to these key words far more urgently than you describing unbear-able pain and how it's impacting your quality of life." But there isn't enough evidence to say how far down the anticapitalist road he might have traveled. Gurwinder told me that when he spoke to Luigi, Luigi didn't seem to have any big solutions. At one point, he even took the side of "top-down" fixes. "He said government should step in and rein in these tech companies," Gurwinder remembered. "But he didn't have a clear idea of how that would happen. So yeah, he didn't come across as a revolutionary. He actually came across more as a Silicon Valley kind of type." That was on May 5, just over three months before the entry in the spiral notebook about the plan coming together: "I finally feel confident about what I will do."

What about technology? Luigi was so enthusiastic about Tim Urban's "Elon Musk Post Series," he posted his five-star review once in 2015 and again in 2018. The series gave a preview of com-ing attractions like killer AI, engineered plagues, particle collider collisions, climate change and a nanobot meltdown that could turn the whole planet into gray goo. Urban saw Musk as the hero who would "back up the humanity hard drive" by putting one million people on Mars. He had godlike plans for melting the Martian polar ice to make oceans and pumping greenhouse gases into its atmosphere to warm things up. By 2040, there could be a Martian city!

Did Luigi still endorse this in 2024? He loved *The Martian*, a popular novel about an astronaut figuring out ways to survive after he's stranded on Mars. Add lab-grown meat and nuclear power and Luigi seems to fit into the eco-modernist camp that supports green technology like electric cars. But he also reposted video clips of Peter Thiel speeches, and Thiel gave up on democracy because the ideas of high-IQ people like him were "not that popular with the crowd," as he put it in his famous essay "The Education of a Libertarian." Real freedom existed only in the realm of technology, Thiel said, because only there can one person affect the fate of our world. The third member of this group is Marc Andreessen, billionaire author of yet another manifesto, *The Techno-Optimist Manifesto*, where he said we have the tools to turn ourselves into supermen if we're brave enough to use them, and if we don't, we're killers, literally; deaths that were "preventable by the AI that was prevented from existing" were a form of murder, he said. Sound familiar?

These three think they're up on the high rungs way above the rest of us, which is where Luigi tried so hard to climb. They're rethinking the world for us poor humans, the NPCs. But Luigi tried to look at different sides. He did that over and over. He cautioned people when they got too extreme.

This was Gurwinder's impression too. "Luigi wasn't a Luddite, but he was somebody who shared Ted's fears about rampant technology because he believed there's nothing to rein in these tech companies. They got too powerful. Governments were afraid of them. So it's like this kind of monster is being born and we can't do anything to stop it."

Which would put Luigi in an exclusive club of two, just him and Ted, except the lines are blurring everywhere now. Three months before Pope Francis died, the Vatican put out a warning that AI could turn humans into "cogs in a machine." Joe Rogan had similar thoughts, even citing Kaczynski by name: "His point was technology is going to destroy the human race and it's going to eventually take over us, and he was right." So did Blake Masters, another Peter Thiel protégé. "This is not an endorsement, but there's a lot of insight there, there's a lot that is correct." JD Vance too: "One has to basically accept that the whole thing is going to fall in on itself."

The wild ones are out there too, dark versions of Luigi. On December 16, twelve days after the Thompson shooting, a fifteen-year-old named Natalie Rupnow killed a student and a teacher and then herself at a school in Wisconsin, leaving behind a manifesto that ended with a quote from one of Ted's rare interviews: "Finally, one learns that boredom is a disease of civilization."

On December 17, the FBI found 150 pipe bombs at a house in Virginia. Police said the homeowner appeared to be a fan of No Lives Matter, an online accelerationist group that seeks, in the words of its manifesto, "the purification of all mankind through endless attacks."

On December 18, an employee at the Anderson Express manufacturing company walked into a staff meeting in a black medical mask and stabbed the company president, who survived. Police said the attack was a possible copycat of Luigi's.

On January 1, 2025, a decorated Green Beret named Matt Livelsberger parked a rented Tesla in the driveway of the Las Vegas

Trump International Hotel, set off a homemade bomb and shot himself in the head. His manifesto said the top 1 percent treated us like cattle, income inequality was outrageous, the number of homeless on our streets was embarrassing and disgusting—so rally around Trump and Musk and "ride this wave to the highest hegemony for all Americans!" He was interested in strength and masculinity and worried about the dangers of advanced technology like "gravatic propulsion systems," the so-far still sci-fi idea of anti-gravity aircraft. It's those blurring lines again, left and right mixing in a delirious swirl. "We've seen a lot of hybrid movements and ideologies, new trends that we can't categorize under the traditional categories," said a RAND Corporation expert in extremism, Bàrbara Molas. They pick and choose: a little neo-Nazism here, a little "Kaczynski-inspired neo-Luddism" there. Everything is accelerating whether we like it or not, sliding faster and faster to the edge. "Musk and Mangione bear a striking stylistic resemblance," wrote Adam Gopnik in *The New Yorker*. "The appetite for romantic destruction is the flip side of the desire for authoritarian order."

This is a world where Max Wilbert and Andrew Anglin agree, at least on Luigi. It's no coincidence that Republican support for big business has dropped to levels almost as low as Democrats' in the last three years alone.

A wake-up call is what Livelsberger called it in his manifesto, echoing Guy Debord: "Americans only pay attention to spectacles and violence. What better way to get my point across than a stunt with fireworks and explosives?" He ended with tactical advice:

Military and vets move on DC starting now. Militias facilitate and augment this activity. Occupy every major road

along fed buildings and the campus of fed buildings by the
hundreds of thousands. Lock the highways around down
with semis right after everybody gets in. Hold until the purge
is complete.

Four weeks later, a woman from Massachusetts was arrested
with two Molotov cocktails and multiple knives. She told police
she wanted to kill the "Nazi" Speaker of the House or the secretary of defense or maybe the secretary of the treasury. She said
she was facing a terminal illness and had been "thinking about
this because of Luigi Mangione."

That closed out January, the first month of 2025, less than two
months after Brian Thompson's death.

•

Now we've entered a time of fables, the mad king, the monster in
the maze and the emperor without clothes. I can no longer affirm
the social order like the responsible seventy-year-old grandpa I
was only six months ago. My own government is trying to silence universities and law firms, banning books, whitewashing
history and snatching people off the streets. Within months of
the 2024 election, Republicans in Congress and state legislatures
introduced forty-one bills to punish protest. In England, climate
protesters have gotten four- and five-year prison sentences just for
blocking roads. The Civil Liberties Union for Europe's annual report in 2025 found protest under threat "particularly for climate
activists and pro-Palestinian demonstrators" in France, Germany,
Greece, Hungary, Ireland, the Netherlands and Romania. Right
on time, in March, *Mother Jones* published an article called "As
Europe Criminalizes Environmental Protest, Some Activists Turn

to Sabotage," documenting pipeline attacks in England, France and Germany.

JFK said, "Those who make peaceful revolution impossible will make violent revolution inevitable."

And Brian Thompson, the apple-cheeked Iowa farm boy who rose to such impressive success? He seems to have been a good dad, at least judging by his decision to move into a house just a mile away from his ex-wife and kids when his marriage broke up. And yes, his hands were pretty far from the actual bloodshed. But he was making $10 million a year and sold $15 million in stock in what looks very much like insider trading. He presided over an algorithm tweak that kicked medical patients out of rehab after short stays, sometimes long before their doctors recommended. Then there's *United States v. UnitedHealth Group*, which accused him of "knowingly and improperly" canceling a claims verification program in order to boost annual profits by $250 million, which helped the company meet revenue targets it had promised to Wall Street. With all that and a denial rate significantly higher than the closest competitor's, Thompson raised UnitedHealthcare's profits from $12 billion in 2021 to $16 billion in 2023, a 33 percent jump in just two years.

After the death penalty charges pushed Luigi's fundraiser past a million dollars, his supporters explained why they'd chosen to contribute. "I am disturbed by what the government is doing to you," said one, giving Luigi $5,000. "For them, it was and always will be about protecting the 1%."

Max Wilbert compared Luigi to Jessica Reznicek, the Catholic Worker serving eight years for arson attacks on an oil pipeline. Reznicek said, "I was indicted on malicious use of fire when the whole world's burning."

But in the end, pinning down Luigi's motive misses the point. Luigi's elusiveness is what really matters. For a growing group of Americans who seem to be vibrating with existential anxieties, he became a screen onto which they projected their fears and dreams of an era when the center didn't hold, when AI and social media made science scary, when climate change challenged our faith in progress and change itself somehow became impossible and unstoppable at the same time. These Americans don't fit neatly into left or right, but even if they see the problems and solutions in radically different ways, they're united in their hunger to fix the world. They feel helpless and responsible at the same time. They're desperate to break free.

On Luigi's twenty-seventh birthday, May 6, 2025, he wrote a list of twenty-seven things he was grateful for, starting with his friends and a joke: "(2) My family, for [REDACTED—my personal life is none of your business!]" From there he reached wide, thanking his cellmate, his pen pals, independent media creators, the Disposable Heroes of Hiphoprisy, artists in general and even the prison staff, "who are nothing like what 'The Shawshank Redemption' or 'The Stanford Prison Experiment' had me to believe." On politics, he thanked the conservatives "who fiercely conserve the aspects of our society that make us great" and also the liberals "who liberate us from the outdated aspects of our society that prevent us from being greater."

In the trail Luigi left behind, he traced out the lurching path so many of us have taken through the flood of ideas that washed over our civilization with the arrival of the internet, much of them false or dumb, some of them fresh or unexpected, as we searched for new structures of meaning to stabilize our unsettled world. We're still searching, and probably will be for a long time to come. But this is what history teaches us: Robin Hoods come with a beautiful promise, to escape into the deep forest where we can be free. They arrive in times of social turmoil, when the people are suffering and nothing makes sense anymore—in the time of fables, when we can be heroes or monsters.

ACKNOWLEDGMENTS

Writing a book on a tight deadline is a desperate adventure with an uncertain outcome, but I was lucky enough to have Laurie Abraham by my side. She's so loving and supportive and also happens to be a great editor who worked at *Mirabella*, *Elle*, *New York*, *The Atlantic* and *The Economist*. Julia Richardson and Rachel Jepsen were an incredible help, comfort and inspiration (they're my daughters), and an extra thanks to Rachel for her egg-on-face-saving last-minute edit. Thanks also to Katherine Potter, their mom, who helped with babysitting and moral support and in so many other ways, now and always. To David Granger, who kept me employed at *Esquire* for almost twenty years and then brought me one more gift in this book. To Mark Warren, the editor who guided me through so much of the reporting that informed these pages. To Ali Flint for her endless enthusiasm and compassion, which gave this book a good, hard push and always makes the world a little brighter. To Priscilla Painton, Sean Manning and the whole team at Simon & Schuster for their thoughtful support, and to Nick Tabor for his meticulous research assistance. To the angels of my distant past who helped me find a path through the years of struggle: Olga Matich, Barb Page and Susan Lyne. And Gay Storm, Anne Sterling, June McKemy, John House, Chris Furst, Mark Hess, Barry Blitt, Rob Shepperson, Ann Douglas, Bill Ruhlmann—running out of breath, exit music playing—and Tom Brewster! And finally all thanks to Elijah, the Joy-Bringer. It's always a pleasure to call him my grandson, but I think calling myself his grandfather is better. The world is his now. For better or for worse, with all my prayers, this book is for him.

NOTES

Chapter 1: Magic Island

3 "The industrial revolution and its consequences": Ted Kaczynski, "Industrial Society and Its Future," *Washington Post*, September 22, 1995, https://www.washingtonpost.com/wp-srv/national/longterm/unabomber/manifesto.text.htm.

3 "Boredom, demoralization, low self-esteem": Kaczynski, "Industrial Society and Its Future."

4 "The bigger the system grows": Ted Kaczynski, "Letter to M.K.," April 26, 2017, https://web.archive.org/web/20180216134040/https://www.wildwill.net/blog/2017/04/26/letter-ted-kaczynski-to-m-k/.

5 "Nothing that stood out at the time": Yasmeen Hamadeh, "Roommate Spills How Luigi Mangione Discovered Unabomber's Manifesto," *Daily Beast*, December 10, 2024, https://www.thedailybeast.com/roommate-spills-how-luigi-mangione-discovered-unabombers-manifesto/.

5 After 240,000 years as hunter-gatherers: Tim Urban, *What's Our Problem?* (Claymont, DE: What But Why, 2023), "The Big Picture" (unnumbered chapter).

8 from computer pioneers like Bill Joy: Bill Joy, "Why the Future Doesn't Need Us," *Wired*, April 1, 2000, https://www.wired.com/2000/04/joy-2/.

8 to public intellectuals like Paul Kingsnorth: Paul Kingsnorth, "Dark Ecology," *Orion* and *Dark Mountain*, 2014, https://www.paulkingsnorth.net/dark-ecology.

9 "The eco-fascist narrative": Andrew Silke, "Eco-Terrorism: Assessing Current Threats and Trends," *Poole Re Monthly Threat Update*, July 2022, https://assets.poolre.co.uk/sitefiles/2022/08/COH_J013147-Pool -Re-MTU-July-2022-C3.pdf.

Chapter 2: Dear Ted

13 I interviewed Craig Venter: "Craig Venter," *Esquire*, October 2008.

13 I spent time with some of the guys: "How Much Better Can We Stand to Be?," *Esquire*, May 2015.

13 I did a story about a scientist: "Eric Loewen," *Esquire*, December 2009.

13 I covered the 2009 UN Climate Change Conference: "Don't Need a Weatherman to Know Which Way the Wind Blows," *Esquire*, April 2010.

13 I covered the 2015 Climate Change Conference in Paris: "James Hansen Goes Nuclear," *Esquire*, May 2016.

13 I traveled along the Keystone Pipeline: "Keystone," *Esquire*, September 2012.

13 a story about a dot-com tycoon: "Inside the Race to Hack the Human Brain," *Wired*, November 16, 2017, https://www.wired.com/story/inside -the-race-to-build-a-brain-machine-interface/.

13 Then I met another young man: "Children of Ted," *New York*, December 11, 2018, https://nymag.com/intelligencer/2018/12/the-unabomber-ted -kaczynski-new-generation-of-acolytes.html.

14 I found a Fox News piece: Keith Ablow, "Was the Unabomber Correct?," Fox News, June 25, 2013, https://www.foxnews.com/opinion/was-the -unabomber-correct.

17 "His reliance on his own intuition": Kelefa Sanneh, "Intellectuals for Trump," *New Yorker*, January 1, 2017, https://www.newyorker.com /magazine/2017/01/09/intellectuals-for-trump.

Chapter 3: Dear Luigi

19 There seems to be some question: Janna Brancolini, "Luigi Mangione: Cops Might Have Planted Critical Piece of Evidence," *Daily Beast*, December 10, 2024, https://www.thedailybeast.com/luigi-mangione -denies-2-key-details-in-unitedhealthcare-ceo-brian-thompson-killing -complaint/.

20 a reporter tallied the day's total: Nia Prater, "The People Cheering the UnitedHealthcare CEO Shooting," Intelligencer, *New York*, December 6, 2024, https://nymag.com/intelligencer/article/unitedhealthcare-ceo -shooting-celebrations.html.

25 Here's muckracking filmmaker Michael Moore: Michael Moore, "A Manifesto Against For-Profit Health Insurance Companies," December 13, 2024, https://www.michaelmoore.com/p/a-manifesto-against-for-profit-health.

25 "The brazen public murder of Brian Thompson": Leana S. Wen, "The Only Appropriate Reaction to the Murder of a Health Insurance CEO," *Washington Post*, December 12, 2024, https://www.washingtonpost.com /opinions/2024/12/12/murder-thompson-unitedhealthcare-ceo-response/.

26 Megan McArdle dismissed the whole controversy: "The CEO Killing Is Awakening the 'Yes, but . . . ' Brigade," *Washington Post*, December 12, 2024, https://www.washingtonpost.com/opinions/2024/12/12/united -health-care-shooting/.

26 "Raskolnikov with a silver spoon": Bret Stephens, "Brian Thompson, Not Luigi Mangione, Is the Real Working-Class Hero," *New York Times*, December 12, 2024, https://www.nytimes.com/live/2024/12/04/opinion /thepoint.

27 "a threshold-breaking attack": Robert A. Pape, "What the Glorification of Luigi Mangione Reveals About America," *New York Times*, December 12, 2024, https://www.nytimes.com/2024/12/12/opinion/luigi -mangione-united-healthcare-ceo-shooting.html.

27 "liberal wackos are treating suspected killer Luigi Mangione": Will Neal, "Laura Ingraham Fumes at Fans 'Salivating' over Luigi Mangione's Looks," *Daily Beast*, December 11, 2024, https://www.the dailybeast.com/fox-news-host-laura-ingraham-fumes-at-fans-salivating -over-luigi-mangiones-looks/.

27 "putting a smiley face on assassination": Charlie Nash, "Hannity Confronts Taylor Lorenz, Tells Her She Has 'A Missing Chip,'" Mediaite, April 16, 2025, https://www.mediaite.com/media/tv/youre-putting-a -smiley-face-on-assassination-hannity-confronts-taylor-lorenz-tells-her -she-has-a-missing-chip/.

27 "This is a warning that if you push people": Molly Farrar, "'People Can Be Pushed Only So Far': Warren Reacts to Killing of Health Care CEO," boston.com, December 11, 2024, https://www.boston.com/news/politics /2024/12/11/people-can-be-pushed-only-so-far-warren-reacts-to-killing -of-health-care-ceo/.

27 "It's like you feel cool saying it": JRE Moments, "Luigi Mangione: American Hero or Crazed Gunman?—Joe Rogan & Tim Dillon," YouTube video, December 22, 2024, https://www.youtube.com /watch?v=6C9y16eORCc, at 5:26.

27 "The EVIL Revolutionary Left": Ben Shapiro, "The EVIL Revolutionary Left Cheers Murder!," YouTube video, December 6, 2024, https://www.youtube.com/watch?v=GeRnWYn-GTQ.

27 "Mangione's murder of Thompson": Branco Marcetic, "Luigi Mangione's Anger Wasn't Neatly Ideological," *Jacobin*, December 11, 2024, https://jacobin.com/2024/12/luigi-mangione-unitedhealthcare-thompson-ideological.

28 the "drooling," as the *New York Post* put it: Matthew Sedacca and Georgia Worrell, "Meet the Besotted Groupies Sending Love Letters, Commissary Money to Accused UnitedHealthcare CEO Assassin Luigi Mangione," *New York Post*, December 21, 2024, https://nypost.com/2024/12/21/us-news/meet-the-besotted-groupies-sending-love-letters-commissary-money-to-accused-united-healthcare-ceo-assassin-luigi-mangione/.

29 "I would not touch those gorg curls": Vanessa Friedman, "Objectifying the Accused," *New York Times*, December 11, 2024, https://www.nytimes.com/2024/12/11/style/luigi-mangione-uhc-social.html.

29 "*Time*'s Sexiest Alleged Murderer of the Year": Trish Bendix, "Jimmy Kimmel: America's 'Going Nuts' over a Murder Suspect's Abs," *New York Times*, December 11, 2024, https://www.nytimes.com/2024/12/11/arts/television/jimmy-kimmel-luigi-mangione.html.

29 "I mean, take away the hair": *The Daily Show*, "Michael Kosta on UHC CEO Shooting Suspect Luigi Mangione," YouTube video, December 11, 2024, https://www.youtube.com/watch?v=Ickf4gcCWa8, at 8:52.

29 At the Network Contagion Research Institute: Alex Goldenberg (@AlexWGoldenberg), "The dynamic we are observing is eerily similar to what happens on platforms like 4chan, 8chan, and Discord, where perpetrators of targeted violence are celebrated," X, June 11, 2025, 11:34 a.m., https://x.com/AlexWGoldenberg/status/1867246689586688191.

29 "Someone in that building": Cory Doctorow, "Radicalized," *American Prospect*, December 9, 2024.

30 "The press is calling me to ask": Moore, "A Manifesto Against For-Profit Health Insurance Companies."

30 tried to wave the white flag: Andrew Witty, "UnitedHealth Group C.E.O.: The Health Care System Is Flawed. Let's Fix It," *New York Times*, December 13, 2024, https://www.nytimes.com/2024/12/13/opinion/united-health-care-brian-thompson-luigi-mangione.html.

31 CEOs' requests for security: Liz Nagy et al., "Surge in Executives
    Hiring Personal Security After United Healthcare CEO Murder," ABC 7
    Chicago, February 4, 2025, https://abc7chicago.
    com/post/surge-exec
    utives-hiring-personal-security-united-healthcare-ceo-brian-thompson
    -murder/15862275/.

31 "I think all of us are taking a step back": Michele Gershberg and
    Michael Erman, "Health Execs Reckon with Patient Outrage After
    UnitedHealthcare Killing," Reuters, December 11, 2024, https://www
    .reuters.com/business/healthcare-pharmaceuticals/health-care-execs
    -seek-better-understand-patient-outrage-after-unitedhealthcare-2024-12
    -11/.

32 *ProPublica* ran a piece: Annie Waldman, "UnitedHealth Is Strategically
    Limiting Access to Critical Treatment for Kids with Autism," *ProPublica*,
    December 13, 2024, https://www.propublica.org/article/unitedhealthcare
    -insurance-autism-denials-applied-behavior-analysis-medicaid.

32 CNN did a piece about a woman: Tami Luhby, "'No One Should
    Have to Be Fighting Cancer and Insurance at the Same Time,'" CNN,
    December 12, 2024, https://www.cnn.com/2024/12/12/business
    /us-health-care-insurance-frustrations/index.html.

33 According to the Senate Permanent Subcommittee on Investigations:
    "Refusal of Recovery: How Medicare Advantage Insurers Have Denied
    Patients Access to Post-Acute Care," U.S. Senate Permanent Subcommit-
    tee on Investigations, October 17, 2024, https://www.hsgac.senate.gov
    /wp-content/uploads/2024.10.17-PSI-Majority-Staff-Report-on-Medicare
    -Advantage.pdf.

33 A Federal Trade Commission study showed: Federal Trade Commis-
    sion, *Specialty Generic Drugs: A Growing Profit Center for Vertically
    Integrated Pharmacy Benefit Managers*, Second Interim Staff Report,
    FTC, January 2025, https://www.ftc.gov/system/files/ftc_gov/pdf/PBM-6b
    -Second-Interim-Staff-Report.pdf.

33 Emerson College released a stunning survey: "December 2024 National
    Poll: Young Voters Diverge from Majority on Crypto, TikTok, and CEO
    Assassination," Emerson College, December 17, 2024, https://emerson
    collegepolling.com/december-2024-national-poll-young-voters-diverge
    -from-majority-on-crypto-tiktok-and-ceo-assassination/.

34 YouGov conducted a survey: "Health Insurance & Murder of Brian
    Thompson," YouGov, December 15, 2024, https://d3nkl3psvxxpe9
    .cloudfront.net/documents/Health_Insurance___Murder_of_Brian
    _Thompson_poll_results.pdf.

34 The next day, *Newsweek* published: Sean O'Driscoll, "Luigi Mangione Prosecutors Have a Jury Problem: 'So Much Sympathy,'" *Newsweek*, December 18, 2024, https://www.newsweek.com/luigi-mangione-jury -sympathy-former-prosecutor-alvin-bragg-terrorism-new-york-brian -thompson-2002626.

Chapter 4: Kindred Spirits

37 After serving five years in prison: "Brick by Brick: An Interview with Scott Crow," *Earth First! Journal*, June 2014, https://www.scottcrow.org /brick-by-brick.

38 Tre Arrow, a militant activist: Michael Scarpitti, "'Most Wanted' Eco-Terror Arrest," NBC News, March 15, 2004, https://www.nbcnews.com /id/wbna4534715.

41 The protesters occupied a building: Chris Kraul, "WTO Meeting Finds Protests Inside and Out," *Los Angeles Times*, September 11, 2003, https:// www.latimes.com/archives/la-xpm-2003-sep-11-fg-wto11-story.html.

43 "This fight isn't over cats": E. J. Montini, "No Big Cats in Arizona Fit to Roar for the Lions," *Arizona Republic*, March 18, 2004.

Chapter 5: The Arraignment

50 someone dug up Luigi's Reddit account: Dani Blum and Emily Schmall, "The Debilitating Toll of Back Pain," *New York Times*, December 10, 2024, https://www.nytimes.com/2024/12/10/well/back-pain-mangione .html.

51 "The target is insurance": Emma Bowman, "Federal Murder Charge Against Mangione Could Mean Death Penalty in CEO Killing," NPR, December 19, 2024, https://www.npr.org/2024/12/19/nx-s1-5234272 /mangione-ceo-killing-charges-notebooks.

51 "This investor conference is a true windfall": Bowman, "Federal Murder Charge Against Mangione Could Mean Death Penalty in CEO Killing."

Chapter 6: Gamification

59 The membership included: Gurwinder Bhogal, "My Conversations with Luigi Mangione," *Free Press*, December 23, 2024, https://www.thefp .com/p/conversations-with-luigi-mangione-alleged-killer-brian -thompson.-sad-climatologists-0815/.

61 Although it centers on an act of violence: Gurwinder Bhogal, "Why Everything Is Becoming a Game," *The Prism*, April 20, 2024, https://www .gurwinder.blog/p/why-everything-is-becoming-a-game.

Chapter 7: Peak Hope

69 "climate change, deforestation": Paul Kingsnorth, "Why I Stopped Believing in Environmentalism and Started the Dark Mountain Project," *The Guardian*, April 29, 2010, https://www.theguardian.com/environment/2010/apr/29/environmentalism-dark-mountain-project.

70 "The end of the human race": Though this quotation is often attributed to Emerson, it seems to be apocryphal.

70 "a rope tied": Friedrich Nietzsche, *Thus Spoke Zarathustra: A Book for All and None*, trans. Walter Kaufman (New York: Penguin, 1978), 14.

71 "the year of peak hope": Paul Kingsnorth, "Life vs the Machine," *Orion*, 2019, https://www.paulkingsnorth.net/machine.

71 "most important international gathering": Nicholas Stern and George Monbiot, "Copenhagen Climate Conference: Emission Impossible," *The Guardian*, November 29, 2009, https://www.theguardian.com/environment/2009/nov/30/stern-monbiot-copenhagen-deal.

71 a senior scientist named Gavin Schmidt: Author interview with Schmidt, May 2016.

72 "hide the decline": Fred Pearce, "How the 'Climategate' Scandal Is Bogus and Based on Climate Sceptics' Lies," *The Guardian*, February 9, 2010, https://www.theguardian.com/environment/2010/feb/09/climategate-bogus-sceptics-lies.

72 "This is not a smoking gun": Andrew C. Revkin, "Hacked E-Mail Is New Fodder for Climate Dispute," *New York Times*, November 20, 2009, https://www.nytimes.com/2009/11/21/science/earth/21climate.html.

72 Michelle Malkin issued her snap judgment: Michelle Malkin, "The Global Warming Scandal of the Century," MichelleMalkin.com, November 20, 2009, https://www.unz.com/author/michelle-malkin/2009/11/20/the-global-warming-scandal-of-the-century/.

73 "Communicating with the public": Andrew C. Revkin, "Climate Expert Says NASA Tried to Silence Him," *New York Times*, January 29, 2006, https://www.nytimes.com/2006/01/29/science/earth/climate-expert-says-nasa-tried-to-silence-him.html.

73 "I had been using the first line": TED, "James Hansen: Why I Must Speak Out About Climate Change," YouTube video, March 7, 2012, https://www.youtube.com/watch?v=fWInyaMWBY8, at 5:29.

74 The best known was Steven Milloy: Paul D. Thacker, "At Fox News, a Pundit for Hire," *New Republic*, January 27, 2006.

78 "I've recently been reading": Paul Kingsnorth, "Dark Ecology," *Orion*, January–February 2013.

80 "You just can't imagine how upset I was": Theresa Kintz, "Interview with Ted Kaczynski," *Green Anarchist Magazine*, https://web.archive.org /web/20070227174419/http://www.primitivism.com/kaczynski.htm.

Chapter 8: Such Ruthless Honesty

81 But a bomb could "kill innocents": Dalia Faheid, Michelle Watson, Bonney Kapp, John Miller, and Dakin Andone, "Gun CEO Killing Suspect Luigi Mangione Had upon Arrest Matches Shell Casings from the Crime Scene," CNN, December 11, 2024.

82 "Our responsibility is immense": Tim Urban, *What's Our Problem?* (Claymont, DE: What But Why, 2023), "The Big Picture" (unnumbered chapter).

82 the "primitive mind" of tribalism: Urban, *What's Our Problem?*, chapter 1.

82 He "turned the conservative platform": Urban, *What's Our Problem?*, chapter 4.

83 "social justice fundamentalism": Urban, *What's Our Problem?*, chapter 5.

83 "Accusations of cultural appropriation": Urban, *What's Our Problem?*, chapter 6.

84 Urban goes into prominent cases: Urban, *What's Our Problem?*, chapter 7.

85 a prominent cardiologist crunched numbers: Donovan Harrell, "Med School Professor Removed by UPMC as Fellowship Director over White Paper," *University Times*, August 11, 2020, https://www.utimes.pitt.edu /news/med-school-professor.

86 society is "structured in a way": Abby Goodnough and Jan Hoffman, "The Elderly vs. Essential Workers: Who Should Get the Coronavirus Vaccine First?," *New York Times*, December 5, 2020.

87 according to a recent Pew poll: Rachel Minkin, "Views of DEI Have Become Slightly More Negative Among U.S. Workers," Pew Research Center, November 19, 2024, https://www.pewresearch.org/short-reads /2024/11/19/views-of-dei-have-become-slightly-more-negative-among-us -workers/.

87 "In the chaos of exponential progress": Urban, *What's Our Problem?*, "Changing Course" (unnumbered chapter).

90 "If I imagine the Venn diagram circles": David Wallace-Wells, "Can Anyone Make Sense of Luigi Mangione? Maybe His Favorite Writer,"

New York Times, December 18, 2024, https://www.nytimes.com/2024/12/18/opinion/luigi-mangione-writer-tim-urban.html.

Chapter 9: Psychological Issues

93   his "humility, kindness and affability": Dan Diamond et al., "Luigi Mangione 'Had So Much to Offer'—Now, He Is a Murder Suspect," *Washington Post*, December 10, 2024, https://www.washingtonpost.com /nation/2024/12/10/luigi-mangione-life-school-family-back/.

94   He was "always keeping everybody's energy up": Lorena O'Neil, "The Life and Mystery of Luigi Mangione," *Rolling Stone*, March 9, 2025, https://www.rollingstone.com/culture/culture-features/luigi-mangione -united-healthcare-ceo-shooting-suspect-1235290609/.

95   One post talked about: Luigi Mangione, "IAT—Religion," Luigi Mangione: Stanford AI, July 17, 2015, https://luigimangionestanford .wordpress.com/2015/07/17/iat-religion/.

95   Another grudgingly consented: Luigi Mangione, "Facebook Stalks Me," Luigi Mangione: Stanford AI, July 20, 2015, https://luigimangionestanford .wordpress.com/2015/07/20/facebook-stalks-me/.

95   "I believe we should continue": Luigi Mangione, "Tech vs. Nature," Luigi Mangione: Stanford AI, July 28, 2015, https://luigimangionestan ford.wordpress.com/?s=psychology.

Chapter 10: Down the Dark Mountain

106   "shot, quartered, and fed to the pigs": Robin McKie, "Death Threats, Intimidation and Abuse: Climate Change Scientist Michael E. Mann Counts the Cost of Honesty," *The Guardian*, March 3, 2012, https:// www.theguardian.com/science/2012/mar/03/michael-mann-climate -change-deniers.

107   A British journalist suggested the electric chair: James Delingpole, "An English Class for Trolls, Professional Offense Takers and Climate Activists," *The Telegraph*, April 7, 2013.

112   "consistent with a 2 degrees C scenario": Terry Macalister," Shell Accused of Strategy Risking Catastrophic Climate Change," *The Guardian*, May 17, 2015, https://www.theguardian.com/environment/2015/may/17/shell -accused-of-strategy-risking-catastrophic-climate-change.

112   "professionally depressed": John H. Richardson, "When the End of Human Civilization Is Your Day Job," *Esquire*, July 20, 2018, https:// www.esquire.com/news-politics/a36228/ballad-of-the-sad-climatolo gists-0815/.

Chapter 11: Existential Concerns

118 "He scrunched his nose": Gurwinder Bhogal, "My Conversations with Luigi Mangione," *Free Press*, December 23, 2024, https://www.thefp.com/p/conversations-with-luigi-mangione-alleged-killer-brian-thompson.

Chapter 12: I Wanted to Be the Lenin

131 an article he wrote for Dark Mountain: John Jacobi, "Ted Kaczynski and Why He Matters," Dark Mountain Project, May 6, 2016, https://dark-mountain.net/ted-kaczynski-and-why-he-matters/.

131 "Day by day": Samuel Butler, *The Note-Books of Samuel Butler* (New York: E. P. Dutton & Company, 1926), 39.

131 "a carefully reasoned, artfully written paper": James Q. Wilson, "In Search of Madness," *New York Times*, January 15, 1998, https://www.nytimes.com/1998/01/15/opinion/in-search-of-madness.html.

131 "As difficult as it is": Bill Joy, "Why the Future Doesn't Need Us," *Wired*, April 1, 2000, https://www.wired.com/2000/04/joy-2/.

Chapter 13: Best Regards, Ted

139 A magazine called *First Things*: Elliot Milco, "Searching for Ted Kaczynski," *First Things*, September 26, 2017, https://firstthings.com/searching-for-ted-kaczynski/.

139 "Obviously," Halpern said: John H. Richardson, "Children of Ted," *New York*, December 11, 2018, https://nymag.com/intelligencer/2018/12/the-unabomber-ted-kaczynski-new-generation-of-acolytes.html.

140 "The necessary conditions": Jamie Bartlett, "The Next Wave of Extremists Will Be Green," *Foreign Policy*, September 1, 2017, https://foreignpolicy.com/2017/09/01/the-green-radicals-are-coming-environmental-extremism/.

140 the 2017 report on domestic terrorism: Lisa N. Sacco, "Understanding and Conceptualizing Domestic Terrorism: Issues for Congress," Congressional Research Service, December 29, 2023, p. 11, https://www.congress.gov/crs-product/R47885.

141 Of the 2,700 investigations the FBI pursued: Federal Bureau of Investigation and Department of Homeland Security, *Strategic Intelligence Assessment and Data on Domestic Terrorism*," report, FBI and DHS, October 2022, p. 20, https://www.dni.gov/files/NCTC/documents/news

_documents/2022_10_FBI-DHS_Strategic_Intelligence_Assessment_and
_Data_on_Domestic_Terrorism.pdf.

Chapter 14: Dark Ecologists

144 "civilization is killing the planet": Derrick Jensen, preface to *Deep Green Resistance: Strategy to Save the Planet* (New York: Steven Stories Press, 2011), 11.

151 "A few radical environmentalist groups": Sean Fleming, "Searching for Ecoterrorism: The Crucial Case of the Unabomber," *American Political Science Review* 18, no. 4 (2024): 1986–99.

Chapter 15: Fan Mail

156 The moderators even told members: yowhatupmom, "Out of an abundance of caution, r/FreeLuigi will return to only using initials (LM) when discussing the case due to Reddit's new safety rules," Reddit, March 7, 2025, https://www.reddit.com/r/FreeLuigi/comments /1j5tj74/out_of_an_abundance_of_caution_rfreeluigi_will/.

156 "Imagine that I'm placing my hands": Lauren Davidson Ibarra, "Recap of My Week in NYC Covering & Attending the Luigi Mangione Hearing," An Astonishing Achievement, February 24, 2025, https:// laurendavidsonibarra.substack.com/p/recap-of-my-week-in-nyc -covering.

157 "a club with a strict bouncer": Mia Sato, "The Long Wait for a Glimpse of Luigi," *The Verge*, February 22, 2025, https://www.theverge .com/law/617946/luigi-mangione-unitedhealth-ceo-february-hearing -protest.

158 "one of the most iconic photos": Ibarra, "Inside the Luigi Mangione State Criminal Hearing."

Chapter 16: Going Full Luigi

167 "turned out to be God-shaped": Bari Weiss, "Why an Eco-Warrior Left the Movement—and Became a Christian," *Free Press*, March 30, 2024, https://www.thefp.com/p/weekend-listening-paul-kingsnorth.

167 "nationalist," "heteronormative" and "neocolonial": Out of the Woods, "Lies of the Land: Against and Beyond Paul Kingsnorth's Völkisch Envi-ronmentalism," libcom.org, March 31, 2017, https://libcom.org/article /lies-land-against-and-beyond-paul-kingsnorths-volkisch-environment alism.

167   "rethinking Christianity in a new way": Rod Dreher, "Kingsnorth—
'Living in Wonder' Weekend," Rod Dreher's Diary, October 17, 2024,
https://roddreher.substack.com/p/kingsnorth-living-in-wonder-weekend.

Chapter 17: Countdown

175   "I want some time to Zen out": Mike Baker et al., "Months Before
C.E.O.'s Killing, the Suspect Went Silent. Where Was He?" *New York
Times*, December 12, 2024, https://www.nytimes.com/2024/12/12/us
/luigi-mangione-gunman-united-healthcare-shooting.html.

Chapter 18: Accelerate!

185   "There is a whole movement of people": Andrew Anglin, "No One Is
'Against Vigilante Justice on Principle,'" Daily Stormer, December 13, 2024,
https://dailystormer.in/no-one-is-against-vigilante-justice-on-principle/.

186   Anglin grew up in a big house in Columbus, Ohio: Luke O'Brien, "The
Making of an American Nazi," *The Atlantic*, December 2017, https://
www.theatlantic.com/magazine/archive/2017/12/the-making-of-an
-american-nazi/544119/.

186   "Ted Kaczynski was right": "Andrew Anglin," Southern Poverty Law
Center, n.d., https://www.splcenter.org/resources/extremist-files/andrew
-anglin/.

188   "I don't have a message to the fans": Scott Bixby, "Trump Says of
Campaign Sacrifice: 'I Gave Up Two Seasons of Celebrity Apprentice,'"
The Guardian, May 4, 2016, https://www.theguardian.com/us-news
/2016/may/04/cnn-interview-donald-trump-celebrity-apprentice.

188   "We interpret that as an endorsement": O'Brien, "The Making of an
American Nazi."

188   "I hate hearing about 'innocent people'": "Atomwaffen Division,"
Southern Poverty Law Center, https://www.splcenter.org/resources
/extremist-files/atomwaffen-division/.

189   "Not to withdraw from the process": Gilles Deleuze and Félix Guattari,
Anti-Oedipus: Capitalism and Schizophrenia (New York: Viking, 1972),
239–40.

189   "no distinction to be made": Nick Land, "A Quick-and-Dirty Introduction to Accelerationism," *Jacobite Magazine*, May 25, 2017, https://web
.archive.org/web/20170526141715/http://jacobitemag.com/2017/05/25
/a-quick-and-dirty-introduction-to-accelerationism/.

190   "When the lifeboat is full": Pentti Linkola, *Can Life Prevail?* (Wewels-
burg Archives, 2009), 92.

190   Linkola also loved Ted's "planned, thoughtful model": Linkola, *Can Life Prevail?*, 111.

191   "Power grids are attractive": Elisha Ebrahimji, "What Is Acceleration-ism, the White Supremacist Ideology Promoting Power Station Attacks," CNN, November 8, 2024, https://www.cnn.com/2024/11/08/us/accelera tionism-meaning-manifesto-theory-accelerationist.

195   "It's obvious at this point": Eliezer Yudkowsky, "MIRI Announces New 'Death with Dignity' Strategy," LessWrong, April 2, 2022, https://www .lesswrong.com/posts/j9Q8bRmwCgXRYAgcJ/miri-announces-new-death -with-dignity-strategy.

196   a tech executive named Oliver Habryka: Oliver Habryka, "My Tentative Best Guess on How EAs and Rationalists Sometimes Turn Crazy," LessWrong, June 21, 2023, https://www.lesswrong.com/posts /HCAyiuZe9wz8tG6EF/my-tentative-best-guess-on-how-eas-and -rationalists.

Chapter 19: Propaganda of the Deed

197   Thompson's murder was "an act of political violence": "Attorney General Pamela Bondi Directs Prosecutors to Seek Death Penalty for Luigi Mangione," news release, Office of Public Affairs, U.S. Department of Justice, April 1, 2025.

197   "By seeking to murder Luigi Mangione": "4.1.25 Statement from Karen Friedman Agnifilo," Luigi Mangione Legal Defense Information, April 1, 2025, https://www.luigimangioneinfo.com/statements/4-1-25-statement -from-karen-friedman-agnifilo/.

198   "Defendant's conduct has directly led": Brief, *People v. Luigi Mangione*, IND-75657-24, New York State Supreme Court, March 25, 2025, 6.

200   "lying in wait": "Affirmation in Response to Defendant's Omnibus Motion," *People v. Luigi Mangione*, June 4, 2025, 18.

201   "Any UHC worker": "Affirmation in Response to Defendant's Omnibus Motion," 33.

201   "imagine the merchant's strongbox": Barbara Tuchman, *A Distant Mirror: The Calamitous Fourteenth Century* (New York: Alfred A. Knopf, 1978), 38.

201   In 1358, in a French village: Tuchman, *A Distant Mirror*, 13–14.

201   "After ten or twelve of them": Tuchman, *A Distant Mirror*, 185.

202   "in accordance with his means": Juliet Barker, *England, Arise: The People, the King & the Great Revolt of 1381* (London: Little, Brown, 2014), 130–31.

202 "heryn a tale or song": Alice Blackwood, "By Words and by Deeds: The Role of Performance in Shaping the 'Canon' of Robin Hood," in *Robin Hood and the Outlaw/ed Literary Canon*, ed. Alexander L. Kaufman and Lesley Coote (New York: Routledge, 2019), 51–68.

203 "The law locks up the man or woman": James Boyle, "The Second Enclosure Movement and the Construction of the Public Domain," *Law and Contemporary Problems* 66, nos. 1–2 (2003): 33–74.

204 "In 1649, to St. George's Hill": Leon Rosselson, "The World Turned Upside Down" (song), Digger Archives, https://www.diggers.org/english _diggers.htm#World_Upside_Down.

204 "to starve is more criminal": Thomas Paine, "Case of the Excise Officers," 1772, Thomas Paine Historical Association, https://www .thomaspaine.org/works/essays/other/case-of-the-excise-officers.html.

205 "A few men in the right": James D. Webb, ed., *The Life and Letters of Captain John Brown* (London: Smith, Elder, and Company, 1861), 114.

205 Emerson called him a "new saint": George Willis Cooke, *Ralph Waldo Emerson: His Life, Writings, and Philosophy* (Boston: James R. Osgood, 1881), 140.

206 "Freedom without socialism": Mikhail Bakunin, "Stateless Socialism: Anarchism," in *The Political Philosophy of Mikhail Bakunin: Scientific Anarchism*, ed. G. P. Maximoff (Glencoe, IL: Free Press, 1953), 294–301.

206 "a Brutus stab by the tormented": Alexander Berkman, "Autobiographical Sketches," in *Prison Blossoms: Anarchist Voices from the American Past*, ed. Miriam Brodie and Bonne Buettner (Cambridge, MA: Harvard University Press, 2011), 19–30.

207 Berkman thought it was a mistake: Paul and Karen Avrich, *Sasha and Emma: The Anarchist Odyssey of Alexander Berkman and Emma Goldman* (Cambridge, MA: Harvard University Press, 2012), 166.

207 "a mere particle of a machine": Emma Goldman, *Anarchism and Other Essays* (New York: Dover, 1969), 54.

207 "radical flank effect": Andreas Malm, *How to Blow Up a Pipeline* (New York: Verso, 2021), chapter 1.

Chapter 20: The Dear Ted File

210 I outlined a study: Max Brosig et al., *Implications of Climate Change for the U.S. Army*, report, United States Army War College, 2019, p. 1, https://climateandsecurity.org/wp-content/uploads/2019/07/implications -of-climate-change-for-us-army_army-war-college_2019.pdf.

210 It was especially worried about the power grid: Brosig et al., *Implications of Climate Change for the U.S. Army.*

212 Using a scale of one to seven: Michael Bang Petersen, Mathias Osmundsen, and Kevin Arceneaux, "The 'Need for Chaos' and Motivations to Share Hostile Political Rumors," *American Political Science Review* 117, no. 4 (2023), 1486–505.

214 Some blame schizophrenia: Alston Chase, "Harvard and the Making of the Unabomber," *The Atlantic*, June 2000, https://www.theatlantic.com /magazine/archive/2000/06/harvard-and-the-making-of-the-unabomber /378239/.

215 "Gen Ed delivered to those of us": Chase, "Harvard and the Making of the Unabomber."

Chapter 21: Saint Luigi

218 the poor in America are taught to hate themselves: Kurt Vonnegut Jr., *Slaughterhouse-Five, or The Children's Crusade* (New York: Dell Publishing, 1969), 111.

220 AI could turn humans into "cogs in a machine": *"Antiqua et Nova*: Note on the Relationship Between Artificial Intelligence and Human Intelligence," Vatican, Dicastery of the Doctrine of the Faith and Dicastery for Culture and Education, January 28, 2025, https://www.vatican.va /roman_curia/congregations/cfaith/documents/rc_ddf_doc_20250128 _antiqua-et-nova-en.html.

220 "This is not an endorsement": Ronald J. Hansen, "Who Is Blake Masters? Here's What to Know About the Arizona Republican," *Arizona Republic*, August 4, 2022, https://www.azcentral.com/story/news/politics /arizona/2022/08/04/who-blake-masters-republican-candidate-running -senate/10231501002/.

220 "One has to basically accept": Jason Wilson, "He's Anti-Democracy and Pro-Trump: The Obscure 'Dark Enlightenment' Blogger Influencing the Next US Administration," *The Guardian*, December 21, 2024, https:// www.theguardian.com/us-news/2024/dec/21/curtis-yarvin-trump.

221 "We've seen a lot of hybrid movements": Ali Winston, "The Violent Rise of 'No Lives Matter,'" *Wired*, March 12, 2025, https://www.wired .com/story/no-lives-matter-764-violence/.

221 "Musk and Mangione bear a striking stylistic resemblance": Adam Gopnik, "The Gilded Age Never Ended," *New Yorker*, February 24, 2025, https://www.newyorker.com/magazine/2025/03/03/the-gilded-age -never-ended.

223 "Those who make peaceful revolution impossible": John F. Kennedy, "Address on the First Anniversary of the Alliance for Progress," American Presidency Project, March 13, 1962, https://www.presidency .ucsb.edu/documents/address-the-first-anniversary-the-alliance-for -progress.

223 "I was indicted on malicious use of fire": Rekha Basu, "Jessica Reznicek Is No Terrorist. But the Longtime Activist Is Going to Serve Time as One," *Des Moines Register*, July 25, 2021, https://www.desmoines register.com/story/opinion/columnists/rekha-basu/2021/07/22/dakota -access-pipeline-dapl-iowa-climate-activist-jessica-reznicek-prison -sentence-not-terrorist/7955826002/.

INDEX

antivaxxers, 64
Anton, Michael, 122, 190
Anxious Generation, The (Haidt), 182–83
Ape That Understood the Universe, The: How the Mind and Culture Evolve (Stewart-Williams), 2, 123, 170
Arab Spring, 114
architecture, modern, 176–77, 178
Arizona Game and Fish Department, 43, 47
Atassa (journal), 130, 165
atomic bomb, 5
Atomwaffen Division, 185, 188

Bakunin, Mikhail, 206
Bankman-Fried, Sam, 56, 195
Bartlett, Jamie, 140
Barton, Joe, 107
Beat Generation, 40
Benedict Option, The (Dreher), 167
Bennet, James, 84
Bennett, William J., 139
Berger, J. M., 191
Berkman, Alexander, 90, 206, 207
Biden, Joe, 87, 118
Biocentric (blog), 143
biological weapons, 5
biotechnology, 79, 132
birth rates, decline of, 178, 192, 196
Black Lives Matter, 83, 86, 141
Black Panthers, 90
Boemeke, Isabelle, 124
Bondi, Pam, 197, 198
Boston, Briana, 22
Box, Jason, 105–6, 111, 112, 113–16
Bragg, Billy, 12
Brand, Russell, 64

Brockman, John, 51
Bronze Age, enthusiasts for, 211, 213
Brooklyn Metropolitan Detention Center, 56
Brown, John, 205–6
Buddhism, 95, 100
Buehler, S. M., 141–42
Bush, Sam, 160–61
Butler, Samuel, 131

Cabrera, Abe, 135, 163–66
"cancel culture," 84–85
cancer treatments, health insurance and, 24, 33, 57
"Can Technology Replace Nature?" (Kahn), 95
Can't Hurt Me (Goggins), 170
capitalism, 175, 189, 218
carbon dioxide, 113
Carlson, Tucker, 64, 176, 177
Carnegie, Andrew, 206
Carnegie, Dale, 100
Cato Institute, 72, 79
Center for Biological Diversity, 46
Chase, Alston, 214–15
chestnut trees, disappearance of, 134
"Children of Ted" (Richardson), 55–56
Christianity, 95, 175–76
Cigna, 33
Civilization (video game series), 99
Civilization and Its Discontents (Freud), 14
climate change, 16, 69, 123–24, 127, 165, 183, 218; Arctic carbon release and, 105–6; as challenge to faith in progress, 224; climate communication, 112; "Climategate," 72–73, 77;

ABOUT THE AUTHOR

JOHN H. RICHARDSON is the author of *My Father the Spy, In the Little World* and *The Vipers' Club*. His work has appeared in *Esquire, Premiere, New York, The Atlantic, The New Republic, Wired, GQ, Mother Jones* and various other magazines, along with many newspapers and anthologies, including *The Best American Crime Writing, The Best American Magazine Writing* and *The O. Henry Prize Stories*. He lives in the Hudson Valley with Laurie Abraham, who is doing better these days, thank you.